LIFE IS RICH

HOW TO CREATE LASTING
WEALTH

NATE SCOTT

Life Is Rich: How To Create Lasting Wealth

Copyright © 2014

Published in the United States by

ISBN 978-1-07579-878-8

Cover by Steve Wilson

Formatting & Layout by Chris Ott

Insight Publishing Company

707 West Main Street, Suite 5

Sevierville, Tennessee 37862

Disclaimer: *This book is the result of my personal experience, education, and knowledge about making money, losing money, saving money, investing money, and protecting money. The views and opinions expressed in this book are for the sole purpose of guiding people to make educated decisions about their financial affairs and are not written by a certified financial planner. As the author of this book, I do have an MBA, I have completed an executive financial planning program, and I have worked as a licensed financial advisor. I am no longer a practicing financial advisor, and I no longer hold the following licenses: Series 7, 66, Life, Health, and Annuity, Mortgage, and Rea l Estate. Therefore, you are advised to consult a certified financial planner and/or tax consultant with any questions you have regarding any information found in this book, as well as any additional questions you may have regarding managing your personal finances.*

DEDICATION

Matthew 13:44-46 "The kingdom of heaven is like treasure hidden in a field. When a man found it, he hid it again, and then in his joy went and sold all he had and bought that field. 45 Again, the kingdom of heaven is like a merchant looking for fine pearls. 46 When he found one of great value, he went away and sold everything he had and bought it."

To God Be the Glory

To my children, Nadia and Tre' Scott, I love you. Always remember that you are my inspiration and my greatest asset. I am excited by the growth I see in you each day. You both are amazing. Love, honor and respect your mother because she ensures that you have a balanced life. Thank you Dana L. Scott for all that you do. I appreciate our ability to effectively co-parent. That's truly a blessing.

To Susan Berrier-Pacetti, you entered into my life unexpectedly, and I am glad you did. You are an amazing lady. I appreciate your strength and courage. Thank you for your love and support throughout this process. You are forever apart of my heart and story.

To all of my family and friends and specifically those that were there when I needed support - Nathaniel Scott, Sr., Lucille Wooten, Reverend Delmons White, Nellar and Tommy Lonon, Brodie Waters, Barrye L. Price, Michael Miner, Jamar Scott, and George Harris. Thank you for being there when it happened to me.

To my mentors, mentees, and encouragers, specifically, Renita Menyhert, John Terhune, James Bayfield, Josh Rogers, Charles Hawkins, Pastor Edward Weston, the Brigade, BJ Webb & Team Gotta Body, Miguel Camargo, the Visalus community, the Quantum Leap community, and the West Point community. You recognized my gifts and challenged me to share them with the world.

Lastly, I dedicate this book to you, the reader. Thank you for allowing me to be a person of value and positive influence in your life. Serving you gives meaning to my life. Please send me a note and let me know the breakthroughs that you experience as a result of reading this book and pay it forward so that others may come to understand that "Life Is Rich": Nate@AskNateScott.com.

Be Blessed.
Nate

TABLE OF CONTENTS

1 Peter 5:2-4 "2Be shepherds of God's flock that is under your care, serving as overseers-not because you must, but because you are willing, as God wants you to be; not greedy for money, but eager to serve; 3not lording it over those entrusted to you, but being examples to the flock. 4And when the Chief Shepherd appears, you will receive the crown of glory that will never fade away."

*Leaders have a responsibility. I have chosen **1 Peter 5:2-4** as a "call to action" to leaders/influencers (the led) – Pastors (Church members), Teachers (Students), Business Owners (Employees), Coaches (Athletes), Network Marketers (Team), Financial Advisors (Clients), CPA (Clients), Attorneys (Clients), Parents (Children), Government (Constituents), Military (Veterans, Service Members and their families).*

John 10:6-11 "6 This parable spake Jesus unto them: but they understood not what things they were which he spake unto them. 7 Then said Jesus unto them again, Verily, verily, I say unto you, I am the door of the sheep. 8 All that ever came before me are thieves and robbers: but the sheep did not hear them. 9 I am the door: by me if any man enter in, he shall be saved, and shall go in and out, and find pasture. 10 The thief cometh not, but for to steal, and to kill, and to destroy: I am come that they might have life, and that they might have it more abundantly. 11 I am the good shepherd: the good shepherd giveth his life for the sheep."

*We must learn to recognize the dangers that prevent us from having the life we desire. I have chosen **John 10:6-11** to show the distinction between good and bad. For the believer, we are promised the opportunity to have an abundant life. Unfortunately, most people do not know how to recognize an opportunity. As a servant-driven leader, I am called to teach people how-to.*

Psalm 23:1-6 "23 The Lord is my shepherd; I shall not want. 2 He maketh me to lie down in green pastures: he leadeth me beside the still waters. 3 He restoreth my soul: he leadeth me in the paths of righteousness for his name's sake. 4 Yea, though I walk through the valley of the shadow of death, I will fear no evil: for thou art with me; thy rod and thy staff they comfort me. 5 Thou preparest a table before me in the presence of mine enemies: thou anointest my head with oil; my cup runneth over. 6 Surely goodness and mercy shall follow me all the days of my life: and I will dwell in the house of the Lord for ever."

Exodus 35:35 "35 He has filled them with skill to do all kinds of work as engravers, designers, embroiderers in blue, purple and scarlet yarn and fine linen, and weavers—all of them skilled workers and designers."

We must learn to ask "is there a market actively seeking a solution to a problem that I can solve or to fill a desire that I can meet". I have chosen **Exodus 35:35** *as a reminder that God has given all of us talents that we can sell, but that doesn't mean you should start a business. Make yourself a student of business, first. Make sure there's a paying client for your product or service. Develop your business and leadership skills so that you can turn your talent into a real business.*

2 Timothy 3:14-17 "14 But continue thou in the things which thou hast learned and hast been assured of, knowing of whom thou hast learned them; 15 And that from a child thou hast known the holy scriptures, which are able to make thee wise unto salvation through faith which is in Christ Jesus. 16 All scripture is given by inspiration of God, and is profitable for doctrine, for reproof, for correction, for instruction in righteousness: 17 That the man of God may be perfect, thoroughly furnished unto all good works."

John 10:10 "10 The thief cometh not, but for to steal, and to kill, and to destroy: I am come that they might have life, and that they might have it more abundantly."

Luke 14:28-30 "28 For which of you, intending to build a tower, sitteth not down first, and counteth the cost, whether he have sufficient to finish it? 29 Lest haply, after he hath laid the foundation, and is not able to finish it, all that behold it begin to mock him, 30 Saying, This man began to build, and was not able to finish."

Luke 10:23-24 "23 And he turned him unto his disciples, and said privately, Blessed are the eyes which see the things that ye see: 24 For I tell you, that many prophets and kings have desired to see those things which ye see, and have not seen them; and to hear those things which ye hear, and have not heard them."

Matthew 22:17-22 "17 Tell us therefore, What thinkest thou? Is it lawful to give tribute unto Caesar, or not? 18 But Jesus perceived their wickedness, and said, Why tempt ye me, ye hypocrites? 19 Shew me the tribute money. And they brought unto him a penny. 20 And he saith unto them, Whose is this image and superscription? 21 They say unto him, Caesar's. Then saith he unto them, Render therefore unto Caesar the things which are Caesar's; and unto God the things that are God's. 22 When they had heard these words, they marveled, and left him, and went their way."

My personal mission is to live each day principle-centered based upon Biblical teachings and to be a person of value and positive influence in the lives of the people within my circle of influence.

FOREWORD

It's been almost twenty-five years since the first time I ever saw Nathaniel Scott. He was marching, at least that's what it seemed like to me into Speech 100, a public speaking course I was teaching for the University of Maryland in Katterbach, Germany. The majority of my class was soldiers, but these men and women had changed into civilian attire since they were not required to be in uniform. Nathaniel, however, was still dressed in battle dress uniform from that time period. And his looked like he had just picked it up from the cleaners—sparkling clean and neatly pressed. Add the spit shine boots that glowed like mirrors and I knew I had a professional soldier who would give his studies the same dedication he gave the U.S. Army.

I remember wondering if Nathaniel would continue his "strive for excellence" attitude to this course or apply it to more important subjects. This was simply an introductory speaking course required for all college freshmen; but I needn't have worried. Every speech this young soldier was assigned showed a clear demonstration of research about the topic and rehearsed presentations to provide his peers a guaranteed first-class performance.

It wasn't long before I began exploring means to propel Nathaniel into a more challenging atmosphere—one that would complement his exceptional intelligence and provide a solid and meaningful foundation for a promising future. The answer was to encourage him to apply and gain entrance into the United States Military Academy Preparatory School (USMAPS) followed by an appointment to the United States Military Academy at West Point (USMA).

Although somewhat hesitant and unsure about his ability to meet such an extraordinary challenge, due to being away from regular academics since high school, I assured Nathaniel this would not be an issue. I had spoken with his other teachers and company commander who wholeheartedly agreed that the young soldier "has what it takes!" I also explained that the goal of the Preparatory School is to reintroduce and build solid study skills for soldiers who are on active duty and not from a current academic environment.

With the same dedication and persistence to perform his best, the way that Nathaniel exhibited with me, he went on to graduate from the Preparatory School and West Point and earned several awards in academics and leadership. During his last year at USMA he would lead as the United States Corps of Cadets' Third Regimental Commander. As I watched Nathaniel march to and up the platform to receive his degree, I thought that he looked even taller than I remembered.

More admirable accomplishments were forthcoming: graduation from Airborne, Ranger, and Infantry School and serving his country in Korea and with the 3rd U.S. Infantry Regiment (The Old Guard) in Washington, D.C. Nathaniel continued to grow in my eyes with more achievements by continuing his education and pursuing ambitions that continue to leave me overwhelmed. Never have I met anyone so determined to improve himself, follow through on ideas, and turn them out as successfully as Nathaniel.

After reading his book, *Life Is Rich,* I now look at Nathaniel as a truly gifted leader—a man who is willing to share good fortune with others and encourage them to become successful, productive human beings who offer good things to and for the world. Follow this leader's words and see yourself accomplish far more than you ever thought possible.

Col. (ret.) Renita Menyhert, USA

Author of *Army Life: Up Close and Personal*

PREFACE

I know people who make a lot of money, but what are you doing to create wealth? Your answer to that question can be the difference between you experiencing your American Dream or your American Nightmare.

I am the foremost authority on residual income financial planning strategies. To my knowledge, there is no other person documented for teaching real world financial principles with entrepreneurship as the foundation for creating lasting wealth. Nor is there any other person sharing their personal story of how they applied experiences from an untraditional education to become a millionaire cash flowing over $10,000/month before receiving a financial education and entering into the financial services industry as a licensed financial advisor. My story provides a somewhat unique perspective, and it will provide hope and a blueprint for those with a burning desire to own their life. I sit on the same side of the table as you. You can count on me to tell you what the bankers, brokers, bosses, and uplines don't want you to know or are unable to tell you.

I have written this book to be a mentoring guide to help you create a comprehensive financial plan as an entrepreneur. If you have a desire to earn an income of $10,000 or more per month or if you are currently earning an income of $10,000 or more per month AND you want a proven blueprint for becoming a documented millionaire (i.e. Assets minus Liabilities equals Net Worth) within 36 months, then this book is for you. This includes professional athletes, entertainers, entrepreneurs, commissioned salespeople, independent contractors, and network marketers.

In this book, you will discover why and what you need to know about the financial opportunities of becoming an entrepreneur. The first chapters will take you through the process of creating, planning, and then growing your business. Next, I will share some of the many sources available to fund your business as well the best way to structure your affairs. You will explore the different business entities that are available from corporations to limited liability companies. These entities can protect your assets, legally reduce your taxes, and keep your financial affairs private.

The chapter on residual income retirement planning offers a new and innovative approach to solving a problem that most people are in denial about. Finally, you will see how corporations and trusts can be used to fund your retirement needs and how they can be used effectively for estate planning purposes to let you make money, keep money, and pass your assets along to your heirs.

If you have a desire for me to assist you by recommending an advisor or by meeting with your current advisors for a fee, then please schedule a consultation at www.AskNateScott.com or email me at Nate@AskNateScott.com.

As you experience success as a result of this relationship, others will ask you "how did you do it?" I have made it very easy to promote what I do to other people as well. Simply invite them to "Like" www.facebook.com/YourLifeIsRich.

Be Blessed.

One more thing: you can grow even more by inviting others to grow with you.

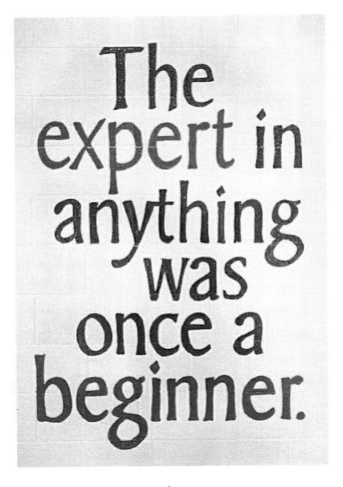

"DAILY HABITS DONE DAILY BUILD CHARACTER"

I am your constant companion.
I am your greatest helper or heaviest burden. I will push you onward or drag you down to failure.

I am completely at your command.
Half of the things you do you might as well turn over to me and I will do them - quickly and correctly.

I am easily managed - you must be firm with me. Show me exactly how you want something done and after a few lessons, I will do it automatically.

I am the servant of great people,
and alas, of all failures as well.
Those who are great, I have made great. Those who are failures, I have made failures.

I am not a machine though
I work with the precision of a machine plus the intelligence of a person.

You may run me for profit or run me for ruin - it makes no difference to me.

Take me, train me, be firm with me, and I will place the world at your feet.

Be easy with me and I will destroy you.

Who am I? I am Habit

INTRODUCTION

My promise is simple: "If you lend me your ear, I'll give you my heart." I truly respect each one of you, and I respect your time. I want to ensure I deliver content that is directly related to what you're trying to get done in your life, and that gives you a little bit more. So how do I get that done? Simply invite them to "Like" **www.facebook.com/YourLifeIsRich**. Can I count on you to do that?

As a former enlisted soldier, Desert Storm Veteran, West Point graduate, and Army Infantry Officer/Ranger, I was committed to teaching my soldiers how to think versus what to think because on the battlefield, I had no idea what specific situation they would face. Therefore, I had to train them to be effective decision makers and leaders independent of me. Throughout the life of our relationship, I want you to always remember that when reading, listening to, or watching me share information. In every situation, I want you to ask yourself, "So what? How do I apply this content to my life on daily basis?

This book is about making money. My objective is to show you that knowledge is the answer to everything you want, and to help you to believe that you will become wealthy by knowing the right things to do and doing them.

But before we get too far into that, I'd like to speak with you about something that I think is a little more near and dear to your heart—ways to achieve financial independence. How many of you would like to be financially independent? Well, what does that mean to you to be financially independent? Please take a moment and answer that on a blank sheet of paper.

It seems that we each have a different definition of what financial independence means and that's okay. I want you to start and end this book knowing one thing: the American dream of financial independence is alive and doing well. And whatever that dream might mean for you, you can have it if you simply take the time to learn how to get it.

My intent is to teach you what I believe is the foundation for creating your personal MBA in any industry at any time. In your mind, you may be thinking Master's in Business Administration, but I am speaking of a Massive Bank Account. Isn't that what you really want and need in order for you to live the life that you desire? If you are currently unemployed or underemployed, I want you to do what you do as far as the process of looking for a job; however, I want you to develop into the person others want to hire. More importantly, be willing to hire yourself.

The first step in that process is that we need to stop working so hard. Is that good news? I know that I am already telling you things that are contrary to what you've been told all your life. What were you told about working hard? Get a good education and you work hard and everything will be just fine. But what happened? We did get a good education. We did work hard but let me ask you something. How many people do you know who are hard workers? How many of those people are wealthy? Evidently working hard doesn't work. I rest my case.

What you've got to learn to do today is to work smart. Now, I know you've been told that before but in today's context, working smart means getting involved in something that will give you income.

1. It might mean getting involved in something that will give you some tax breaks.
2. It means getting involved with something that will build a savings for you.
3. It means getting involved with something you could own—something that would go up in value.
4. It means getting involved with something you don't have to have so much of your money involved in.

Now, would you like to get involved in a program like that? If so, then connect with me at **www.facebook.com/YourLifeIsRich**.

Begin with the end in mind. The pages of this book have valuable information, so you will need to have your pen and paper ready because I believe it will help you. This is, in my opinion, not much different than when I served as a soldier. I'm saying that the same way I fought to give people the opportunity to participate in this country and to get all the benefits, I'm still fighting to give people freedom. That is still my core character and who I am. So now, with that said, I want to commend and thank any past and current military service members—my brothers and sisters in arms—for their service.

I know you're reading this book, but I still want to get you involved. I want you to play full out. Are you ready?

I want you to settle into this book, and I am going to ask you some questions that require your participation. I encourage you to respond as I ask you to, even if it feels weird. Trust me, it'll make your reading experience a learning experience versus pure entertainment.

By a show of hands, how many of you have a college degree? Okay. Keep your hands up if you have a master's degree. How about an MBA? Okay, hands down.

I did my undergraduate studies at West Point in Engineering and Sociology. I have an MBA from George Washington University, and Financial Planning from Georgetown.

By a show of hands, how many of you guys are not from the state of Florida? Okay, hands down. I'm originally from a small town outside of Savannah, Georgia.

By a show of hands, did any of you ever play any organized, competitive, team sports at any level? Okay, hands down. When I was growing up, I had the aspiration of playing college basketball. When I graduated from high school, I turned down my academic scholarships because my dream wasn't to go to college. My dream was to play college basketball and to travel. I chose to enlist in the Army and to go to Germany. As soon as I got to my unit, I started playing sports and enrolled in college classes. It has been said that most people die at twenty-five and wait to buried at sixty-five. As I reflect on the choice I made at eighteen years old to pursue my dreams, I realize the significance of that early decision.

Even with that experience of failure, I still had the goal of playing college basketball. Because I began with the end in mind, I enlisted in the Army to continue to work on my game. You see, it was something I wanted. So I commend those of you who have athletic spirit because that's a character trait you can turn into a competitive advantage.

I started thinking about financial independence as a tenth grader in high school, beginning with the end in mind.

So, I want you to take note of a couple of things: Number one, write down the name of the book, *The Cash Flow Quadrant* by Robert T. Kiyosaki and Tim Wheeler. Have you read that book? Have you read *Rich Dad Poor Dad* by Robert Kiyosaki? Okay, if you've put them down on your sheet of paper, then add them to your To Read List.

The things I'm going to give you are the tools. I'm going to tell you the things that have enabled me to do what I've done, all with the foundation of God, but I want to let you know there are some things you've got to do in the physical ream as well. And so, the things I'm sharing are also within your reach.

Okay, the next thing I want you to do is begin with the end in mind. Add Stephen Covey's book, *The Seven Habits of Highly Effective People*, to your To Read List. I consider myself to be an inspirational teacher, not a motivational speaker. I'm not trying to give you a rah-rah session, but you will be inspired. You will have marching orders, but you will know what you need to do to move forward in order to seize those great opportunities this great country has to offer. I won't coddle you, I won't hold your hand, I won't pat you and tell you it's going to be okay—unless it's true.

So, I will hug you. I will tell you it's okay . . . because I believe it's true, but you've got to believe it, too. In the book, *Rich Dad, Poor Dad,* by Robert Kiyosaki, he speaks about the four-quadrants. Right now, for the most part, everyone is striving to be in the "E" quadrant. That's what a job market's about. You've also got the self-employed. You may be a person who would be okay with doing some things as an independent contractor, maybe setting up your own office. That's great.

I want you to realize that you have options other than being in the "E" quadrant. "E" is the employee, "S" is the self-employed, "B" is the business owner, and "I" is the investor. You can generate income from multiple sources. In fact, I strongly recommend that you do.

Wouldn't you say we've realized over the last few years that there have been some uncertain times? By a show of hands, how many of you have been unexpectedly laid off? Will you let that happen again? It's easy to say you won't, so what are you doing to protect yourself?

My last corporate position was as the CFO of a mortgage and Real Estate technology company. We were listed as number 155 on INC500's fastest growing companies. We shut our doors in December of 2007. December 2007 was the last time I had a job. By a show of hands, how many of you have been unemployed as long as I have been? I understand.

Well, one thing you have to do is decide to put something in place to give yourself that backstop for Plan B. Are you a homeowner? Do you have homeowner's insurance? Do you own a car? Do you have car insurance? Do you have a job? Do you have insurance for your income? Do you have a Plan B? It might be okay for a little while, but eventually that dries up. I recommend that you run a stress test on your income to see how long you could withstand an unexpected life change such as a job loss, income reduction, divorce, death, or illness.

If working smart is going to be involved in this, then why hasn't it worked? I think two of the reasons most people haven't reached financial independence is because of taxes and inflation. What is the inflation rate right now? What were you paying for a loaf of bread ten years ago? What are you paying today? It's the same product. It's not any better. It's not any worse. It just costs a whole lot more. That's inflation, isn't it? Inflation doesn't mean that things become more valuable. It just means that it costs more money to buy the same thing. So we get a pay raise, and we think we're getting ahead. No! We have to make more money to buy the very same thing. That's the effect of inflation. By the way, you make more money to buy the same thing but have you ever noticed that the tax system is based on the more money you make, the higher the tax is? So who do you think is in charge of inflation? The people collecting the higher tax rate, right. The reality is that the government needs more money. To get more money, the taxes must go up. There are only three classes of people in this country:

1. the poor people,
2. the people in the middle
3. the wealthy people.

Do you believe that the government will raise the taxes on the poor? What would be the benefit? How do you help the country by taxing people who don't have any money?

How many of you believe they will raise the taxes on the wealthy people? Well, there are only three classes of people. Where do you think the tax increases are going to be focused? Who do you know are those paying federal income taxes right now? How many of them do you think would like to stop? If you don't want to pay any more in federal income taxes, it seems to me that you have one of two choices:

1. Become rich or
2. Become poor.

Which would you prefer? I made a decision to become wealthy in the tenth grade of high school.

Inflation is like trying to walk up an escalator that's going down. The value of a dollar keeps going down, and we're working harder and harder trying to keep up. And as you try to get ahead, then the taxes hit you. What you have to do is learn a system that allows people to get up out of that system.

Would you like to learn a principle that will make inflation work for you instead of against you? Would that be valuable to you? Now think about what I just said. We have all felt inflation in our wallets. What would happen if inflation worked for you instead of against you? There is a process you can do. In fact, in the book, *Pillars of Success*, I share how I used this process to control more than $5M in Real Estate. Wealthy people have learned it and when you learn it, you hope that the inflation rate goes higher. When wealthy people want the inflation rate to go higher, then guess what happens to inflation? It normally goes up.

Let me share with you that piece of information. In a lot of countries, things are not adjusted for inflation. There is one thing in this country that is not adjusted for inflation and if you know the correct answer, you can become literally filthy rich. What is it that is not adjusted for inflation? Real Estate is not the answer. The answer is *debt*.

Just for clarification, there are two key financial statements that we all should learn to understand: income statement and balance sheet. Income minus expenses equals cash flow; whereas, net worth is the difference between your assets and your liabilities. Debt is a liability that can be turned into an asset, if you know how to do it.

Let me show you what I'm talking about. Here's a very simple plan. Go out and buy a million dollars worth of real estate. If you don't have any money, then borrow it. You have a million dollars worth of real estate and you owe a million dollars. How much equity do you have? Zero.

Now inflation comes along. It costs more money to buy the same thing. Now the price of the Real Estate goes up. What happens to the debt? It stays the same. What's the difference between the value and the debt? Equity. Wealthy people have learned to go into debt. That seems strange doesn't it? You think most wealthy people owe nobody money? No, wealthy people owe everybody. Why? Because debt is not adjusted for inflation but the asset you bought with the debt is adjusted. This means that as the price continues to rise on that asset, the debt remains the same. That principal can make you filthy rich if you just master it.

Here's my story: I was in my last three months of military service when I realized that if I didn't take action right then it would be much more difficult for me to get financing in the immediate future because I would be in between jobs, changing careers. One question bankers typically ask is for a history of income. Knowing this would be a problem, I aggressively began looking for income-producing properties to purchase. During that time I stayed true to the discipline of finding the right property in the right location for the right price.

After looking at listings for more than a hundred properties, I called upon one property in particular and decided to go see it. It met my criteria and I put it under contract. Later during the week, I called on another property and realized that I had called the same phone number earlier—the owner had two different properties on the market for sale. Since I already had one of the houses under contract, I asked the seller about the second property he had listed. I looked at the second property and was able to negotiate a package deal to acquire both properties at a substantial reduction in the asking price. (This is something I always want to do—find something at a good deal—a bargain.)

That one deal saved me more than $125,000. The very next project I looked at, within the next thirty days of putting the first properties under contract, was a forty-unit apartment complex. That complex was located three hours away from where I was living. It was an area I had never heard of, never been to, and had no information about; but I went ahead and called on it. It interested me enough to take the drive up to the location and the numbers made sense so I ended up putting the forty-unit project under contract. Through negotiations with the seller I was able to acquire that property at a discount of more than $100,000 and the seller took back a note of 15 percent of the purchase price. I only put 5 percent into the deal. The forty-unit apartment complex is where most of the cash flow came from. As a result of capital improvements, good management, raising the rents, and decreasing expenses, I was able to increase the value of this income-producing property. Over the fifteen months of holding them, those projects grew in value and provided the foundation for my personal net worth to grow.

Anyone can be a successful Real Estate investor if he or she is willing to get involved and are disciplined enough to find the deal and run the numbers up front versus getting caught up in the emotions of what they think is happening—trend following. I was LUCKY—Labor Under Correct Knowledge. I think that one would find, through just going through the Real Estate section in a library or a bookstore, that individuals who have experienced success have the exact same story but it's worded differently—the principles are exactly the same. We share the exact same philosophy about doing business. The thing about Real Estate is you can be a trader, you can be a growth-and-income person, or you can be strictly an income person. There are many ways a person can make money in Real Estate.

The downside is that individuals don't go in with knowledge. The knowledge doesn't have to be internal; it could be knowledge from external sources also. Individuals jump into it because they hear of the excitement and all the success stories. From an investment standpoint, Real Estate in and of itself is no different than stocks, bonds, and securities. If you go into it with no knowledge, if you go into it haphazardly, you can lose and most likely you will lose your money. You should have an understanding of how to maximize your profits from the following:

- Buying and holding
- Using other people's money (OPM) and other people's time (OPT) and other people's knowledge (OPK)
- Buying, fixing, and selling
- Quick turning, flipping, and wholesaling
- Lease optioning

WEALTH PRINCIPLE: Buy an income-producing asset, then you can afford to borrow the money to buy it with.

Examples:

- Don't buy vacant land. You'd have to pay for it directly because you couldn't afford to borrow the money.
- If you buy a $100K rental house, and the price of Real Estate goes up 10 percent due to appreciation in one year, then the house would cost $110K to buy. That's a profit of $10K. Let's learn a financial term called "Yield." To determine the yield, or rate of return, you get on your money, divide the profit by your cash investment.

When inflation and appreciation comes along, do they know which properties have loans on them and which ones don't? No!

So it goes up at the same amount, doesn't it? So you have the same house, the same year, the same appreciation.

A. Buy the house cash for $100K and get a return of 10 percent (10/100).
B. Borrow $90K and invest $10K to get a return of 100 percent (10/10).

ANSWER: B

Wealthy people have learned that you make more money when you use other people's money (OPM). So even if you have money, don't use it. The people with the *knowledge* understand this.

What I see in today's market is that many people call themselves investors but are, in essence, speculators. I'm particularly referring to the big craze on flipping new construction. I don't get excited about that particular vehicle—it's the objective at the end that drives whether or not I'm in Real Estate or something else, depending on what the overall plan is.

I evaluate all financial decisions based on the *ideal* formula. I ask myself whether or not it passes the test.

- ✓ I = *Income* (money coming in)
- ✓ D = *Deductions* (ordinary & necessary expenses; why did you buy it?)
- ✓ E = Equity Build Up (something I'm building value into)
- ✓ A = *Appreciation* (do you have an asset that is going up in value? Do you "know" what goes up in value?)

L = *Leverage* (Leverage is a principle that wealthy people fully understand and most people have never heard of. Leverage is the insider's secret to creating wealth. Here's the secret: you make more money when you use other people's money. If you are buying an income producing asset (i.e., business, Real Estate, or knowledge to apply), then you can afford to borrow the money).

I would recommend that you determine whether the industry fits into your plan and that you understand the pros and the cons. Once you do that and feel comfortable with it and understand if it is an active or passive investment, then you are ready to invest. If you want to have an active investment, realize that you've got to have systems in place to run it, just like a business. There are enough proven systems out there so you don't have to "reinvent the wheel." Also, there are a lot of guys like me who offer coaching services for a fee. The value we provide is that you get an expert to walk you through the deal. This is the leverage of OPK (Other People's Knowledge). You save time and money by investing in the coaching relationship. "A thousand-mile journey begins with the first step that can only be taken one step at a time." I'll help you start living the life that you've dreamed about.

The people who may be seen as having a "knack" for being successful are people who have done the work at the front side of their success. In other words, they prepared for their success. They worked to reach their success—they've made their own luck.

I just finished reading a book about the difference between a job and work. The difference is a job is something you get paid for. Work is something you do independent of getting paid. A great athlete or a doctor will put in work well before the time he or she earned the designation of professional and the ensuing big paycheck. Likewise, most people who are successful in investing in general have done the work up front. They just make it look easy because what is seen is the end result. The effort that went into preparing for their opportunity is not as visible.

For example, when Magic Johnson was at the top of his game, that's all we saw and all that we expected. The dedication, commitment, and drive he had to succeed were not as visible as his success. The same holds true for him today in business. I guess you can say that Magic has been "lucky," too.

So, let's go ahead and get into the right mental state. My personal mission is to live each day principle-centered based upon Biblical teachings and to be a person of value and positive influence. I am committed to creating a $10 million endowment fund to foster personal growth and entrepreneurship. In order to achieve that, I need to help 100 people earn $100,000 a year, and 100 people build a net worth of $1 million. A hundred times one thousand is one million, and 10 percent of one million is ten million. As a global Internet entrepreneur, business strategist, speaker, author, and coach, I provide an instructional plan, accountability, support, and encouragement in helping people to realize their passion full time.

Repeat the following mantra three times each day for the next ninety days.

- Dramatic wealth is a virtue.
- I am open and receptive to any ideas and people that will help me to achieve my goal of dramatic wealth.
- I am worth $_____/month and I love sharing it with those in need.
- Through perseverance, I am creating the financial dynasty that I so richly deserve.

"You can't get to the future without first going through the present. Take care of today's cash needs before worrying about building an empire."

Life Is Rich
www.AskNateScott.com
904.838.2623

CHAPTER 1
Leadership is the Answer

1 Peter 5:2-4 "2Be shepherds of God's flock that is under your care, serving as overseers-not because you must, but because you are willing, as God wants you to be; not greedy for money, but eager to serve; 3not lording it over those entrusted to you, but being examples to the flock. 4And when the Chief Shepherd appears, you will receive the crown of glory that will never fade away."

Leadership is the most essential element of business. Leadership provides purpose, direction, and motivation in up and down markets. The leader determines the degree to which time and money are maximized, ensures these elements are effectively balanced, and decides how to use both in successfully accomplishing the mission of financial independence.

My military career began as an enlisted soldier, which laid the groundwork for me as a leader. As an enlisted soldier, I was the follower and the doer. After serving three years as an enlisted soldier and after Desert Storm, I went on to West Point. When I graduated, I was commissioned as an Army infantry officer. In this role, I was the leader, teacher, and doer. Fortunately, I had the experience of being the doer first, which gave me immediate credibility as a leader.

One of the people I routinely study is Napoleon Hill. He says that the mastery of procrastination is decision. One of the great things about the military is that it provides an opportunity for young men and women to make and be responsible for decisions.

According to Napoleon Hill, "Accurate analysis of over 25,000 men and women who had experienced failure, disclosed the fact that lack of decision was near the head of the list of thirty of the major causes of failure. This is no mere statement of a theory—it is a fact. Procrastination, the opposite of decision, is a common enemy which practically every man must conquer." He continues on by saying, "Analysis of several hundred people who had accumulated fortunes well beyond the million-dollar mark, disclosed the fact that every one of them had the habit of reaching decisions promptly, and of changing these decisions slowly, if, and when they were changed. People who fail to accumulate money, without exception, have the habit of reaching decisions, if at all, very slowly, and of changing these decisions quickly and often."

You will have an opportunity to test your capacity to reach quick and definite decisions when you finish reading this book, and are ready to begin putting into action the principles that I share.

The principles I learned as an enlisted soldier as well as an officer were modeled after Army Field Manual 22–100—Army Leadership. Application of those principles helped me to be successful throughout my military career as well as in the business world. Here is the framework:

1. BE:
- *Technically and Tactically Proficient:* Can accomplish all tasks to standard that are required to accomplish the mission. In Real Estate, those tasks include market research and analysis, debt management, property management, financial proposal presentation, and capital formulation.
- *Possess Professional Character Traits:* Courage, Commitment, Candor, Competence, and Integrity.

2. KNOW:
- Four major factors of leadership and how they affect each other: those who are led (bank, investors, team, support network), the leader (you or your entity), the situation (market/opportunity), and communications.
- Yourself and seek self-improvement: Strengths and weaknesses of your character, knowledge, and skills. Continually develop your strengths and work on overcoming your weaknesses.
- Your team and look out for their well-being. Train them to think about your objective, take care of their financial needs, and discipline/reward them.

3. DO:
- *Seek Responsibility and Take Responsibility for Your Actions:* Leaders must exercise initiative, be resourceful, and take advantage of opportunities that will lead to victory. Accept just criticism and take corrective actions for mistakes.
- *Make Sound and Timely Decisions:* Rapidly assess situations and make sound decisions. Gather essential information, announce decisions in time for your team to assist you, and consider short- and long-term effects of your decision.
- *Set the Example:* Be a role model for others. Set high, but attainable standards. Be willing to do what you require of your team, and share dangers and hardships with your support network.

- *Keep Your Subordinates Informed*: Keeping your subordinates informed helps them make decisions and execute plans within your intent. It encourages initiative, improves teamwork, and enhances morale.
- Develop a Sense of Responsibility in Subordinates: Teach, challenge, and develop subordinates. Delegation indicates you trust your subordinates and will make them want even more responsibility.
- *Ensure the Task is Understood, Supervised, and Accomplished*: Your team needs to know what you expect from them: What you want done, what the standard is, and when you want it.
- *Build the Team*: Train and cross train your team until they are confident in the team's technical/tactical abilities. Develop a team spirit that motivates them to go willingly and to confidently approach each opportunity.
- *Employ Your Team in Accordance with Its Capabilities*: Know the capabilities and limitations of your team. As a leader you are responsible to recognize both of these factors and employ your team accordingly.

Those are the principles we have in the military. Application of those principles helped me throughout my military career as well as in the business world.

Know your allies—mentors, supportive family, and friends—and know your enemies (those in opposition to your goals and expectations). My allies continuously provide me with emotional support and encouragement. They provide positive reinforcement and constructive feedback. They are not "yes" men or women. They act as my sounding board and enable me to objectively question my thought processes. We share a great deal of respect and admiration for each other. My success is their success and vice versa. These allies have been within my family, my military commanders and peers, my West Point classmates, and my colleagues.

Discipline was a major part of my Army career, but I learned discipline before I joined the service. Fortunately I grew up in a disciplined household. Also, as an athlete, I had a chance to learn discipline early on through the competitive environment of athletics. Often we think about the military as a primary place to learn discipline, but well before I got into the military I had another training ground for discipline. The military just gave me another opportunity to develop and strengthen good habits.

What discipline does is teach one to delay gratification, which has been the cornerstone of my success. It gave me the ability to be forward looking. Knowing my goal routinely enables me to step back and assess the situation, ensuring I do the things most congruent with allowing me to reach my desired outcome versus getting off track because of something immediate. I learned to be more proactive than reactive and only through discipline was I able to do that.

Courage has also been a contributor to my success. Overcoming life's obstacles and making it to the top in all endeavors requires brave actions at some point, as well as the ability to conquer fears. I think that all self-made millionaires have courage because accumulating wealth often requires taking risks, including financial risks. Economic risk-taking is a requirement for becoming financially independent. The benefits of becoming financially independent are greater than the risks often associated with accumulating wealth. Believing this and taking action is courageous in and of itself. The fear of economic failure is not easy to overcome and that's why so few people have the courage to take that leap of faith into the possible.

My faith in God has been essential to my success throughout my life. I was deployed to fight during Operation Desert Storm at the age of nineteen. Prior to deploying, I made a video will that I sent to my family stating I did not know if I would return. Safely returning from that experience gave me an incredible appreciation for life and all that my faith in God has meant to me. I am thankful for my life, my family, and my relationships. I vowed to live life to the fullest and attempt to realize my potential, as God would have me to do. I know that I am and have always been blessed.

Hard work, planning, decisiveness, positive thinking, mind control, and remaining physically, mentally, and emotionally fit are other variables that make up my personal success equation.

When I was in high school, I sat down one day and thought about what I wanted for my life. Actually, I prayed for direction. Early on I knew I wanted to become financially independent and I wanted to achieve wealth, not only for me, but also for my family.

Robert Allen, author of *Multiple Streams of Income,* stated, "Money, by itself, is neither good nor bad, it's neutral. Money is an energy tool. Like a hammer, money can be used to build or to destroy." I believe that understanding money, how to ethically make it, keep it, and share it adds a positive dimension to wealth. Our lives, our relationships, and our happiness improve when there is enough money. Money properly earned and combined with enlightened intentions makes the world a better place. I didn't grow up in a household that had a lot of money or anyone I could emulate from the standpoint of financial well-being. However, I was surrounded by hard-working people. I can remember Dad saying, "Money don't grow on trees." I had a certain phobia up until the age of twenty-seven. Today, I call it "debt phobia."

With that said, I did some very proactive research to identify what things could potentially help me reach my goal of financial independence. I narrowed it down to business and Real Estate. With that thought in mind, as I got older I worked on establishing my credit and increasing my knowledge about investing in general. I then started reading and taking the proactive steps of learning what was necessary to get started in the business of Real Estate. I received my first Real Estate book as a birthday gift in 1998. It was titled, *How to Buy Your Home . . . and do it right,* by Sue Beck. When I was ready, I put a contract on my first home. As Stephen Covey writes in his book *The 7 Habits of Highly Effective People,* I began with the end in mind.

Unfortunately, many people won't realize how ill-prepared they are for retirement until it's too late.

Why do I say that? Because, according to an article I read, sixty-six out of one hundred people age sixty-five, earn less than $30k, 13 percent earn more than $30k, 5 percent earn more than $60k; 1 percent is wealthy and 15 percent are dead.

On a sheet of paper, write down the questions below and answer them:

1. What is your age?
2. What is your desired age to retire, to do what you what to do, when you want to do it, with whom you want to do it, where you want to do it, and for however long you want to do it?
3. How much monthly cash flow do you need for that to happen?
4. How many years do you have to get there?
5. How much do you have invested today?
6. What is the best rate of return you know how to get?
7. Based upon that return, how much do you need to have in cash?

An older man wanted to plant a certain type of tree. A young gardener told the man that this particular tree would take forty years to blossom. The older man replied, "Then, we'd better start this afternoon.'"

The intent of this book is not to make you a financial expert. You don't need an MBA, CFP, or GED. All I want you to do is review your personal numbers to see whether or not you need to make a decision to climb into the wheelbarrow and allow us to help you avoid the disastrous scenario that so many people are facing today.

I want you to ask yourself three important questions:

1. What do I want to get out of this program?
2. Where do I want to be one year from now in my relationships/family life, income, wealth, spiritual life, and so on?

3.   Am I willing to make a choice in my life to change the path I am on right now so that I can position myself for dramatic wealth?

Assuming a 5 percent rate of return:

- If you need an extra $500 per month, then you'll need an asset of about $120,000.
- If your number is $1,500 per month, then you'll need an asset of about $360,000.
- If your number is $3,000 per month, then you'll need an asset of about $720,000.
- If your number is $5,000 per month, then you'll need an asset of $1.2M.

Practical Application

Now that you know the amount you need to retire, at what age do you want to retire? Let's say 65. How old are you now? Let's say 45. How much do you make a year? Let's say $50,000.

Okay, if my math is correct, you have 240 monthly paychecks left in your working career. According to our previous discussion, you need $500,000 before retirement. Today you have $140,000. We're $360,000 short right now. What is the likelihood that you will have saved $1,500 toward retirement out of each of your last 240 checks? My guess is not likely.

As promised, it's decision time. Here is the plan I recommend that you follow to give you a legitimate shot at meeting your cash flow needs versus having no shot at all.

First, make the decision to contact the person who shared this information with you.

Next, make a decision to be open and receptive to reviewing the information that he or she shares with you and consider the information in the context of your needs and desires.

Lastly, make a decision to do or not to do. There is no try.

Before you go, I'd better warn you. The majority of people who fail to accumulate money sufficient for their needs are generally easily influenced by the opinions of others. They permit the newspapers and the gossiping neighbors to do their thinking for them. Opinions are the cheapest commodities on Earth. Everyone has a flock of opinions ready to be wished upon anyone who will accept them. If you are influenced by opinions, when you reach Decisions you will not succeed in any undertaking, much less in that of transmuting your own Desires into money.

If you are easily influenced by the opinions of others, you will have no Desire of your own. Keep your own counsel when you begin to put into practice the principles I have shared here by reaching your own decisions and following them.

You have a brain and mind of your own. Use it, and reach your own decisions. If you need facts or information from other people to enable you to reach decisions, as you probably will in many instances, acquire these facts or secure the information you need quietly without disclosing your purpose.

Close friends and relatives, while not meaning to do so, often handicap one through opinions and sometimes through ridicule, which is meant to be humorous. Thousands of men and women carry inferiority complexes with them all through life because some well-meaning but ignorant person destroyed their confidence through opinions or ridicule.

"Life is not measured by the number of breaths we take, but by the moments that take our breath away."
-Maya Angelou
(US Poet 1928-2014)

www.AskNateScott.com
904.838.2623

CHAPTER 2
What is the Cash Flow Danger?

John 10:6-11 "*6 This parable spake Jesus unto them: but they understood not what things they were which he spake unto them. 7 Then said Jesus unto them again, Verily, verily, I say unto you, I am the door of the sheep. 8 All that ever came before me are thieves and robbers: but the sheep did not hear them. 9 I am the door: by me if any man enter in, he shall be saved, and shall go in and out, and find pasture. 10 The thief cometh not, but for to steal, and to kill, and to destroy: I am come that they might have life, and that they might have it more abundantly. 11 I am the good shepherd: the good shepherd giveth his life for the sheep.*"

You've invested a lifetime into your work, and when you retire you deserve to enjoy the fruits of your labor. Recently, I read an article that showed sixty-six out of one hundred people age sixty-five had an income of less than $30,000 in retirement. Two generations ago, corporate pensions and Social Security ensured a secure retirement for our grandparents. Today, pension plans have become virtually extinct, shifting the burden of retirement savings away from corporations and onto the employees. Our retirement depends largely, not only on our own ability to save and invest wisely, but also on our ability to plan.

According to an April 2009 report by the Congressional Research Service, in 2007, 47 percent of workers had no retirement savings at all. The rest had very little. Of workers age fifty-five to sixty-four, 69 percent reported household retirement account balances of less than $100,000. Most of these people will be forced to extend their work years or accept living in poverty. There are seventy-seven million Baby Boomers marching toward retirement as we speak. Some are ten years or less away. Unfortunately, most are quite ill-prepared and ill-equipped to make their visions and expectations for retirement come true. They don't know how much to save and to appropriately invest in order to create a portfolio that will last a lifetime of retirement. Only about 25 percent of Baby Boomers are confident about their retirement prospects and are on track for a comfortable retirement. Where is your current life plan taking you? How can the disastrous scenario below be avoided?

Chris and Terri Randall have been together for seventeen years. They raised two kids here in Florida and are now proud grandparents. The tables at their garage sale hold all the odds and ends they've collected throughout the years, and there are some special attachments.

Chris: Well, we're having a garage sale. And we've been here since approximately six o'clock this morning setting up. Hope to sell a few things.

Terri: I love Thomas Kinkade. He's a painter of light, so I started collecting with the Thomas Kinkade music boxes. I also collect dolls. My grandmother started me in that.

But now they hope all of it will be sold.

Terri: It'd make a tremendous difference in our life at this point in time. You know, a hundred dollars makes a big difference. Two bucks?

Chris: Yeah, two bucks is fine.

For twenty years, Chris and Terri Randall had worked for a Fortune 500 financial services company, and they were doing okay. But two years ago June, it all fell apart, and fast, with an unexpected layoff. Now they're on the verge of losing the house they've lived in for almost fifteen years. This garage sale is a last-ditch effort to pay their mortgage.

Chris: I've never been homeless in my life. I've always had a place to hang my hat, so that's the reason why we're here today—to prevent being homeless.

Nate: It's pretty easy for us to look at other people and say that the reason someone's poor is because of the bad decisions that he or she made during the person's life. But, in this economy it's very clear that in thirty days your entire world can change and you could end up on the street.

These are very smart, very well-educated people. They come from good families. I mean, if work ethic was the key to success, then they'd never be in this situation. Their life was good. They were bringing home $10,000 a month after taxes. They were able to sponsor Little League teams and Girl Scout events.

Terri: The bills came in, the bills were paid right on time. Fantastic. No idea what was gonna happen. We figured everything was gonna be fine.

26

During the recession, the Randalls survived the first two rounds of layoffs. They were able to hold on as part of a smaller team working longer hours for less money, but then, the company they worked for merged with a competitor company.

Terri: When it initially happened, I thought, "Well, it's no big deal. We'll just get another account."

Chris: I thought my reputation would get me hired quickly. Being honest and reliable and dependable and hard working . . .

Terri: But, no phone calls. Nothing. We were hoping to retire and start a business that we could turn over to our daughter and keep it in the family. But I guess we should have started when we had the chance.

Chris and I sat down and I said, "It's time for us to go back and look in the fields where we've done work in the past." I'm not applying for anything that I'm not qualified for. I'm trained as a business analyst.

Chris: Accounting and retail management, those are the two words I'm looking for at the moment.

Terri: It's a daily grind. Up in the morning, search, and if there's something in there, I'll apply for it. I do this for five, six hours a day. Every day. Chris has had two interviews since March . . . and I've had none.

Chris: Every time I apply for a job, I write it on the calendar. Here's Bank of America Accounting and Financial Analysis, 7–11 Assistant Store Manager, but I didn't hear anything.

In the last ten months, Chris has applied to more than 150 jobs. For older unemployed Americans, like the Randalls, there's a growing fear that in this lagging economy, they may never get jobs again.

Chris: I hate to blame it, you know, on age because I have the gray hair and gray beard, but maybe that is the reason I'm having so much trouble finding another job.

Since March last year, the Randalls have had virtually no money coming in. They have used up their unemployment benefits. Their savings only carried them for four months. By August, their power was about to be shut off. They couldn't pay their mortgage. And they didn't know where to go for help.

Terri: If you don't know where to search, and you don't know what questions to ask, you're in a black hole, with no ladder.

But after coming across a YouTube video, Terri confided in me via e-mail.

Nate: She told me that they had not found a job, and she was looking for food. That was the first thing they wanted—food.

Terri: He said that, you need to go down and apply for food stamps. Contact any of the other charities. Go to your church or your local churches, get a food basket every week.

Nate: I explained that if you want to pay your electric bill, you'd better get food boxes because food equates to money. So if you're not spending money on food, then you will have money to pay your electric bill. This is the new poor. These are people didn't even know where their local pantry was in their community, and they certainly would never have gone there.

In the last six years, churches and non-profits have had more and more people coming in looking for food or help with rent or utilities. Many have just lost jobs and have never needed help before.

According to the most authoritative thinkers and authors in the United States, in ten years the middle class will be completely gone from North America. It's already left twenty-five major U.S. cities. There will be an ultra-rich class and an ultra-poor class. What happens when twenty million adults turn thirty without a job and twenty million other adult Boomers turn seventy without health insurance?

In a society where 95 percent of all people do not read one book a year, the fact that this situation has been predicted and extensively written about means nothing except to those who read legitimate nonfiction on a regular basis. You will not learn this stuff watching Fox news or CNN or *The Voice* or *American Idol* or the *Real Housewives*.

Clearly, planning for retirement is not something that you do shortly before you stop working. Because of the magic of compounding, the earlier you start, the less you'll have to save on a monthly basis. Lower rates of return or higher inflation, of course, will require a much higher contribution. Unfortunately, most people wait too late to run this analysis and never develop a plan to achieve their financial objectives. An even bigger issue is that most people don't have a level of income to fund their plan.

The good news is if you're reading this information in 2013, you have at least ten years left. The bad news is that most people will wait too long to take action. The purpose of this book is to empower you with practical information to positively turn your financial world upside down. Once you understand the concepts, everything will change for you because you'll be mentally prepared to survive and to thrive.

The unemployment rate in the U.S. during the last seven years has been the highest in the country's history. In fact, unemployed people, frustrated that the government hadn't done more to get people back to work, staged many rallies.

This isn't just happening to Chris and Terri. It's happening to a hundred thousand other people who are trying to get this help, too. My goal is to prepare you to respond just as I trained my soldiers to respond to unseen dangers on the battlefield. This is very personal to me. I see myself in them, and I relive my journey.

How much do you need?

You must determine how much you will need in total by the time you are age sixty-five. Studies indicate that retirees will need between 80 percent and 90 percent of their preretirement income to maintain their current standard of living. So, a reasonable target is one that will provide you with an annual income similar to the income you have now. Then you need to consider a "safe" withdrawal rate. This is the percentage of your retirement nest egg you will withdraw each year during your retirement. Research indicates that, if they have saved enough, retirees can best preserve their assets if their annual withdrawal rate is 5 percent or less. This provides a quick for determining the total amount you need to save by retirement: divide your desired annual income by the withdrawal rate.

So, for example, if you want to target a retirement income of $60,000 per year, you need to save $1.2 million ($60,000/0.05). The following formula can be used to quickly estimate of how much you might need to accumulate as a traditional investor (i.e. Savings, Money Market, Certificate of Deposit, Mutual Funds, Bonds and Stocks) before you can retire.

(Desired Annual Income / Expected Annual Rate of Return) = Approximate Total Principle Amount You Must Have

Anything is possible

Now, I want to end this chapter with an amazing story about a man named Michael Downing. At the end of World War II, Michael Downing was asked to go to Germany to speak to a group of wounded soldiers. Michael made the trip to Germany and as he walked in the room, he saw soldiers who had been shot. There were amputees whose eyes told him they had lost all hope, and he empathized with them.

Michael was a successful businessman. He actually was the president of a very successful bank. As he looked at these soldiers, he started his speech by saying this: "I want you to know that anything is possible. I hope that you dream big dreams because you have a bright future ahead of you, and the potential to achieve anything you desire."

The soldiers weren't in good spirits. They began to boo him. And the booing got so severe that Michael stopped and sat down. He reached down and removed his prosthetic right leg. Then he removed his prosthetic left leg. Then he removed his right arm, and took off his left hand.

You see, what the soldiers didn't know was that when Michael was fourteen years old, he fell from the back of a wagon in a snow storm. By the time his parents realized he was missing and came back to get him, he had severe frostbite requiring the amputation of both legs, his right arm at the shoulder, and his left hand at the wrist. He empathized with the soldiers because he knew what they were going through. He had lost all hope in his life before.

And sitting there—a stump of a man—he started his speech over again by saying, "I want you to know that anything is possible. I hope that you dream big dreams because you have a bright future ahead of you, and the potential to achieve anything that you desire."

Now, I have to imagine that was the greatest speech ever given. Michael's message is what I want to leave you with: Anything is possible. I hope that you dream big dreams because you have a bright future ahead of you, and the potential to achieve anything that you desire.

CHAPTER 3

Nearly Bankrupt and Homeless It Happened to Me

Psalm 23:1-6 "*23 The Lord is my shepherd; I shall not want. 2 He maketh me to lie down in green pastures: he leadeth me beside the still waters. 3 He restoreth my soul: he leadeth me in the paths of righteousness for his name's sake. 4 Yea, though I walk through the valley of the shadow of death, I will fear no evil: for thou art with me; thy rod and thy staff they comfort me. 5 Thou preparest a table before me in the presence of mine enemies: thou anointest my head with oil; my cup runneth over. 6 Surely goodness and mercy shall follow me all the days of my life: and I will dwell in the house of the Lord for ever.*"

After building a book of business as a financial advisor for a global wealth management firm, I accepted a salaried position as Chief Financial Officer of a mortgage and Real Estate company. We were listed as number 155 on INC500's fastest growing companies. It was an amazing experience. We travelled the country empowering Real Estate agents and mortgage professionals to be in business for themselves while leveraging us as their funding source, broker, processor, compliance, and technology arm. The Real Estate agents and mortgage brokers were earning a greater commission than they could anywhere else, and we were earning monthly fees for providing technological services and commissions on transactions.

In addition to my full-time salaried position, I was well positioned because I learned and applied the concepts that I am sharing with you in this book. I had a forty-unit apartment complex in Maryland, three luxury homes in Northern Virginia, a five-bedroom, four-bathroom luxury vacation home near Disney World, a rental townhouse in Jacksonville, my Jacksonville office, and my personal residence. I had a H3 Hummer, a Mercedes Benz SL500 hardtop convertible, and a BMW X5. In total, I had a personal Real Estate portfolio valued at about $5M, invested assets of more than $300,000 and I cash flowed more than $12,000 per month. Financially, life was great.

Then, things took a shift in July 2007, when we got a call from our funding source telling us that they were closing their doors. The economy started getting worse as we started looking to establish new relationships. In order to reduce expenses, we made personnel cuts, and I assumed a role as a consultant in lieu of being laid off. In

December 2007, I was notified that the company was among several mortgage companies that had filed for bankruptcy. That was the last time I had a regular, full-time job. For the next three years, I was able to survive with very little change in lifestyle, but then things took a turn for the worst.

Lest you think my life has been nothing but roses, I will also tell you that not every deal I've done has been successful. I have lost more than a quarter of a million dollars on one deal in one year and all I had to show for it was a judgment. My total debt has been over $4,000,000, and the creditors were calling as if they had my number on speed dial. I have seen my credit score drop from 720 to below 600 in less than 45 days. I have been unemployed or underemployed for more than three years at one time and on the verge of filing bankruptcy. Yes, life happens, so when you find yourself on uneven ground, you have to accept responsibility, assume a defensive position while stabilizing, keep your head up, and persevere.

It was probably the lowest point in my life. How could I be a successful businessman and be broke—financially and personally?

My life was out of balance. My marriage was ending, and for the first time since walking the perimeter in the desert I was unsure if I was going to make it out alive. How could this have happened to me? I was too smart and too educated and too good at what I did to be nearly bankrupt—financially and personally. I had become a millionaire and now it was gone. I was feeling like an utter failure. All of this hits close to home. There is a feeling embarrassment and sometimes you feel like a failure. That's hard.

Fortunately, I was able to make it because of my faith, my mind-set, and help from my family and a couple of friends. I had a safety net, but many people do not have a safety net.

Here's how I came through my storm: I took off for a seven-day retreat. I figured that something was really wrong with me in the way I was living my life. I had become obsessed with making money and doing deals. I had succumbed to the erroneous thought that my self-worth was dictated by my net worth. I was not a great dad and I was a horrible husband. I needed to rebuild my life and start again. The way I described this time is that it was like playing in a basketball game. As I was running off the court at halftime to go to the locker room, I glanced up at the score and I was losing in the second quarter of my life and nearing halftime.

So during my halftime, the question was not, am I going to win this game? The only question was, how am I going to play the second half? After my halftime retreat, which included intense Bible reading, I also read Covey's *The 7 Habits of Highly Effective People,* Eker's *Secrets of the Millionaire Mind,* and Gitomer's *Little Black Book of Connections* I worked out daily and included daily meditation. I emerged with a new outlook and philosophy on my life. Since that day, my personal mission and my objectives have been clearly defined. I had already learned the skills of making money. Recreating it in my life was relatively easy since I know what to do and how to do it.

I have always been interested in teaching, but I always thought that teaching could not afford me the financial rewards I desired. Following a speaking engagement in 2010, I was followed into the hallway by about twenty-five people from the audience who wanted to know if I did other seminars or had other speaking engagements.

I said, "Yes, and I am actively doing research to find exactly what people want to learn today." So, I asked them what they wanted and what it would look like if they could have anything they wanted.

This is a very important lesson. I believe that to make a million or a billion dollars or to have a great relationship, you only need to do three things:

1. Find out what they want.
2. Go and get it.
3. Give it to them.

Every financially successful person or company you can think of has followed this simple three-part formula, which is exactly what I did with these students. I asked them what they wanted and what it looked like. This book is a blueprint to help people in going through or coming out of an unexpected life transition.

My desire is very simple. It is to always give you more value than what you actually invest. It's my belief that you should be able to give your time, your talent, and your treasure if you're a believer. I'm not making an assumption that everyone who experiences me by way of any format is a believer. If you're not, I hope that you get a good feel for me and gain a little bit better perspective of why I do what I do. I hope you get an opportunity to actually engage with me on a one-on-one basis and maybe feel comfortable enough to ask questions as it relates to my beliefs, my faith, and why I serve in the manner in which I serve. That's very important to me because at nineteen, when I walked perimeter during Desert Storm, I said, "Lord, if you allow me to make it back, I'll never waste a day of my life." There is something about being in a life-and-death situation that puts things in perspective.

I have to always let people know "from whence cometh my help." I'm referring to Psalm 121. I have to let people know that because it's a commitment for me. It allows me to never get too haughty. Some of you guys have heard me when I've talked about not forgetting where you came from. Sometimes people get this kind of amnesia. It's as though they forget about what God has actually done for them. Well, I can't do that. So no matter what goes on in my life and what things are lost, whatever is gained, I'm still like this.

I am even keeled because I pray. I'm not defined by things that are happening—those external factors—because it's an inside-out job. Foundationally speaking, everything we go through today is going to be about the inside-out work. If you've ever participated in the "The Daily Habit Call" (www.facebook.com/dailyhabitcall), then you have heard me talk about most people who go through life trying to do in order to have, in order to become. That's why people are quick to ask, "What do you do?" Doing and then switching to doing something else and trying to catch the next great wave. Do something else trying to get to somewhere else right and ends up going through this a cycle of turbulence, not knowing really what and jumping from this to that.

Be, do, have. Be, do, have. Be, do, have. "Be first" because we are human beings. We're not a human doing. We are human beings. We are creators. So being is first and foremost. When you can truly understand and embrace who you are, you're steady and your entire life's purpose is all about self-fulfillment. Then, from there, because you're a human being, what happens is then you are able to actually ask for direction so that you can fulfill the purpose you've been wonderfully designed for. Does that make sense?

If you don't understand at first, you've got to be, then you'll be defined by your circumstances. You start getting things such as a big home, a foreign car, jewelry from Tiffany's, a country club membership, and .then you're defined. Now you're successful because everybody sees you as successful. They can actually put a label on you as being successful; they can just as easily say you're unsuccessful, right? That's the part I want you to reflect on. What I want to let you know is that although you are reading this book, I want you to *experience* it. In order to do that, you must participate. Are you ready to get started?

CHAPTER 4
Becoming an Entrepreneur

Exodus 35:35 *"35 He has filled them with skill to do all kinds of work as engravers, designers, embroiderers in blue, purple and scarlet yarn and fine linen, and weavers—all of them skilled workers and designers."*

Today there is no such thing as a safe company, a secure job, or an established market share. Yet today, entrepreneurship is part of the mainstream in our economy. The global economy has opened up new opportunities and with this a new network of suppliers, distributors, and customers who will compete on a worldwide basis. Electronic highways such as the Internet get almost anyone instant access to people and information throughout the entire world. It also provides small businesses with the chance to compete with the largest companies on a more level playing field.

The bottom line is that businesses are constantly changing, which provides the entrepreneur almost limitless opportunities as never before. During the past decade the number of money-making opportunities that match a person's skills, interests, abilities, and ingenuity has become almost too great to count. According to *Forbes* magazine, there are now 1,426 billionaires—the largest number ever, at a huge jump on the 1,226 counted last year.

Business histories have shown repeatedly that the rewards and advantages of working at home can go far beyond a person's wildest dreams. In fact, it's perfectly possible to launch a small business in your garage, backyard, basement, or room in your home and become a giant corporation. Think about Microsoft, a company that started in a garage and become one of the giants in the world of business. At the same time, think of the companies that used to be Titans of the U.S. economy such as the railways, companies like Bethlehem Steel, and even the auto industry.

At the same time the economy is creating more millionaires every day, other businesses continue to fail. It is estimated that about three quarters of businesses fail within the first couple of years.

This book will reveal the opportunities that are available to you as an entrepreneur. And this chapter will show the strategies that successful entrepreneurs have used to start and build their businesses and companies. These are the fundamentals that one can use to ensure success in starting a business.

First, let's talk about what can make a successful entrepreneur. Many people have summed it up in one word: Passion. Next, you must have an entrepreneurial instinct with an overwhelming desire to have your own business. You must have the passion and dedication to be completely dedicated to your goal. Life is too short to start a business that doesn't give you satisfaction and joy. Through good times and bad times, you will stick with something you love.

One of the most important, fundamental things is having an interest in what you are doing. It is key to the success of your business. Another key component for success is brains. But this is not what you might first think. An entrepreneurial brain doesn't have anything to do with how well you did in school or a piece of paper you hang on your wall. To become a successful entrepreneur, you must have a working knowledge of the business you plan to start before you start it. But the largest part of having entrepreneurial brains is having common sense combined with the ability to see opportunities where others missed them. Think about the people who had the entrepreneurial brains to recognize the opportunity of having a McDonald's franchise in the 1960s. At the same time, whenever the far larger group of people, who were presented the same opportunity passed it by. They're the ones who couldn't spot the value that McDonald's was presenting to them.

We will talk about spotting opportunities in a few minutes, but it is important right at the beginning to talk about what you really *don't* need to be an entrepreneur and that is capital. Many people used lack of money as an excuse to keep them from becoming entrepreneurs. They think that they need hundreds of thousands of dollars—all of it in cash—to start a business. This is not the case at all. But you will need seed money of your own plus sufficient cash to maintain a positive cash flow for at least the first year.

Many businesses can be started on a very small scale with a small investment. Then, as the business grows and you gain experience, cash flow from your business can be used for growth. In some cases, you don't need starting capital to hire staff because you might start by doing everything yourself. The do-it-yourself start is a good way to learn everything about your business. It also makes you better qualified to delegate work to others later on. You can control your risk by placing a limit on how much you invest in your business.

We'll talk more about structuring your business and the right way to attract and keep money later on in this chapter. But the important first step is not to get down on issues of money. You have to look at it yourself first and decide if you really want to be in business. You have to become comfortable with a certain level of risk that you have not experienced as an employee.

You then should think about whether to start any business on a full-time basis or by moonlight. There are some interesting advantages and some pitfalls in starting as a

36

moonlight business—a business you start and operate during your off hours while still working at your current job.

More often than not, the advantages of starting as a moonlighter outweigh the risk. You avoid burning your bridges of earnings including retirement, health, fringe benefits, and vacations. Your full-time job won't suffer as you maintain certain conflict of interest disciplines, including compartmentalizing your current job and your business into completely separate worlds.

There are great advantages for operating a family business the family can run the business while you're at work. You have a built-in organizational structure. You can teach your kids the benefits of being in business.

There are some pit falls to consider in starting a moonlight business, such as the temptation to spend time at your job working on your moonlight business. That's unfair to your regular employer and should not be done under any circumstances. You may need a family member or some trusted person to cover emergencies when you're at your job. Any kind of conflict with your regular work can jeopardize your job and your moonlight business. Being overworked and having the accompanying mental and physical exhaustion can also become a very real problem for moonlight entrepreneurs.

In whatever way you decide to structure your business startup, either on a full time of a part-time basis, the key is to get started. What makes an entrepreneur different from other people is his or her ability to find ideas and follow through with them. Most people are not oriented to do anything at about their ideas, while still others believe it would take too much of their time and money to follow through to completion. This leaves the marketplace wide open to the person who needs to explore any good idea and turn it into profit.

Learn to look around you as you go about your day and learn to write your ideas down. Keep your mind open as you go through each day. What did you notice in the store that would reduce cost or increase sales if some simple procedure were added or something changed? Ideas for improvements are one of the most valuable things you can contribute to a business and at the same time add to your network. To create ideas for improvements, consider every possibility and alternative for the thing you want to improve. Learn to create ideas by evaluating all the different aspects of the product, method, or concept you're interested in. Put your imagination to work. List the things you want to improve. Why should it be improved? Who will benefit from the improvement? What is wrong with it now? Did someone else cause a problem with it? How do you propose to improve it? Exactly what parts need to be improved? Should it be smaller? Should it be larger? Should the color be different? Would more activity help make it better? Could it be combined with something else to make it more practical? Would a basic material work better? Is it complicated? Could it be simplified? Would a substitute be more meaningful? Is it priced too high? Would a change in personnel help the situation? Can the shape be changed to better advantage? Can a new marketing plan make the difference? Is it safe? Can it be mass produced to bring the unit cost down? Should the appearance be changed? Streamlined? Is there an adequate guarantee? What can make it appeal to a bigger audience? Would new packaging or trade name enhance it? Can it be made heavier, lighter, higher, or lower? Can it be franchised? Is there a good maintenance program to back it up? Can financing be simplified?

List ways to increase production, list ways to increase sales, list ways to reduce costs, list ways to increase proficiency, list ways to improve quality and increase profits. The idea behind this process is to get your entrepreneurial brain going. Write down on ideas as they come to mind in every variation you can think. Don't judge the good and bad, just right them down and judge them afterward. You'll stop the flow of ideas if you're critical of your thoughts before you put them on paper.

When you've answered everything you can about the product or concept and know how it fits in with your plans, sit down and evaluate all the details you've written. After you have found or created a good idea, follow it up with questions on what should be your next move in order to do something about it then act.

Remember, take the time to select the business that is just right for you. You will not be penalized for missing opportunities.

The selection process takes a lot of planning and your experience and complete knowledge is vital for your success. Don't tackle businesses that may be too challenging. It's better to identify a one-foot hurdle than to try to jump a ten-footer. Try to identify a business that has long-term economic potential. Following Gratis' advice, go to where the puck is going, not to where it is.

Look for a business that will grow in today's and tomorrow's market. Many small retail stores are no longer in business because huge stores such as Walmart and Home Depot provide choices to the customer often at a cheaper price. Think about your own strength and weaknesses to determine the abilities you have to take in inventory of yourself. Decide what you enjoy doing the most and what you feel you would be good doing. Examine every possibility and include every skill you have, no matter how slight.

Once you have your idea, the next step is to put together a business plan. This is a step business partners often overlook, but it's very important for a number of reasons. First and foremost, it will define and focus your objective using appropriate information analysis. You can use it as a selling tool in dealing with important relationships, including your lenders, investors, and banks. You can use the plan to solicit opinions and advice from people, including those in your intended field of business who will freely give you invaluable advice. Your business plan can uncover omissions and or weaknesses in your planning process.

There is nothing magical about all of these. It usually starts with a simple outline. You put the material together and then you lay out what the first stage of your business should look like.

The first couple of months are crucial for any business. You should write down on paper what needs to come together and what should be the next stage as the business evolves. Then there are other areas such as: What are your plans for marketing? How do you distribute your products? Who's going to sell it? What value are you going to give your products? How will you resell your products or service? What should you avoid in your business plan? Place some reasonable limits on long-term future projections, with long-term meaning more than one year. You're better to stick with a short-term objective and modify the plan as your business progresses.

Too often, long-range planning becomes meaningless because the legality of your business can be different from your initial concept. Avoid optimism. To offset optimism, be extremely conservative in predicting capital requirements, timelines, sales, and profits. Few business plans correctly anticipate how much money and time will be required. Do not ignore spelling out what your strategies will be in an event of business adversities. Use simple language in explaining the issues. Make it easy to read and understand. There's no need to get overly concerned with making up a business plan. It can be as short as a few pages and as long or as complex as you wish. The key point is to get something down on paper that's spells out your idea and makes it clear to others what you're thinking about.

To make it easier, here are five steps that will get you to a worthwhile plan:
1. Write out your basic business concept.
2. Gather all the data you can on the feasibility and the specifics of your business concept.
3. Focus and refine your concept based on the data you have compiled.
4. Outlining the specifics of your business using a what, where, when, why, how, approach might be useful. And number, put your plan in a compelling form so that it will not only give you insights and focus, but at the same time will become a valuable tool in dealing with business relationships that will be very important to you.

Don't let putting together a business plan stop you from starting up your business. Success is about having the courage to begin. It isn't how you start out that's important, what really matters is: do you have the courage to begin?

Now let's look at how you finance your business. As I mentioned before, lacking available cash as a big hurdle to some people when staring their own business. In reality it needn't be. Where do you look for money? The first place to look for financing is right at home. Personal savings should be considered the primary source of funds for starting a business. If you haven't started already, start now to begin accumulating cash through personal savings.

Take an inventory of items you don't need and get rid of them. Sell that extra car, have a garage sale. Sell what you don't need on eBay. Turn to members of your family or close friends who have faith in you and want to see you succeed. Offer to repay them through profit sharing. Go to individuals in your community who believe in you, not those who believe in your bank statements. If you have a good credit history, your banker should consider you. Two other excellent sources would be your local small business administration and chamber of commerce. Your local small business administration has low interest loans available for qualified applicants and your chamber of commerce can assist you with referrals and other helpful information. How much do you need? Think about these things: buying supplies and inventory while waiting to get paid, paying payroll and rent, buying equipment and fixtures, getting a computer. Prioritize those areas where your options are limited to paying in cash and reviewing your alternatives where there maybe another way.

For example, it's not necessary to pay all cash for a delivery truck when you can rent or lease one. Next, review what might serve as collateral for your loans. Some credit is granted on an unsecured basis such as credit cards, but most small business loans are secured by the assets of your business, your personal assets or both. "Unsecured" means that there is no collateral granted for the loan. Examples of unsecured loans are credit cards, unsecured lines of credit such as the offers you get in the mail or from friends or relatives.

A "Secured loan" is defined as assets pledged to secure the payment in the event you're not able to pay. Examples are computers leased, home mortgage, car loan or lease, small business administration loan.

Common types of collateral are equity in your home, accounts receivable, inventory of the business and equipment. Lenders go through an evaluation of the collateral to determine how much they can lend against it. Some key variables as to what kind of loan terms you can get are number of years in business. This is your track record and it is very important. Banks usually require three years, while others are less stringent.

Financial institutions vary in the way they service the public. For example, you would probably not get a car loan and a large corporate loan at the same place. Just as you should start looking around, start thinking about sources of money that are available to you and what the person or people giving you the money want in return.

The first step is to know what your lender wants. A common way is to simply ask. A better way is to ask a friend or business advisor such as your accountant. For a business loan, the most common things are business financial statements, business tax returns, business plan with budget or projection, personal financial statements, and personal tax returns.

The next step is to be ready to answer questions about your business and be ready to highlight your financial performance both in the past and your plan for the future. You'll be more impressive if you have carefully thought out and become familiar with your plan. Bring your accountant if you need help. Be prepared to tell them why you need the money. "I just need the money," does not inspire confidence, or the fact that you have thought it through. Give them some detail about your business. Propose a repayment plan.

Examples of different structures are a line of credit, payable at your discretion but subject to renewal annually by the bank or a term loan payable monthly during a set number of years starting on such and such a date. Most lenders have some flexibility. Potential lenders appreciate that you're thinking about paying them back instead of just getting the money.

Another tip to keep in mind is to be well-dressed and neat in appearance. That pretty much goes without saying but it will definitely reflect positively. Most lenders, including the small business administration, will want to see your business plan.

Keep your lender informed about the status of your business—the good and the bad. If you're unable to make a loan payment on time, call your lender in advance. Advise him or her about the problem and request the extension you need. Explain the sources of repayment. Virtually all lenders will do a personal savings and corporate credit check; be prepared to discuss any prior credit issues or problems.

The best access to a lender is by a referral. Lending is a people business. Have your accountants, lawyer, or a friend introduce you to a lender. The first thing that will spook lenders or investors is the theory you are "all show rather than substance." Avoid giving the impression of being an over-optimistic, "pie in the sky" operator. As a start-up, don't plan to spend money on expensive entertaining. Your lender will be more interested in knowing how their money is being used to grow your business.

Do not depend on a bank to lend you money to start a business. Most small-businesses are funded by personal savings. Make a shrewd appraisal to minimize your risks and to limit losses to a predetermined limit. Your suppliers and vendors can be sources of financing. For example, if you need an illuminated sign for your storefront, the company you've contract with to make the sign may provide financing so you can make monthly payments rather than pay cash. Examples are: longer payment terms, advertising and marketing assistance, furnishing or financing of equipment, signs, or inventory, advertising, and a promotional program. They want your business!

Be aware of the different types of investors who come to you saying they want to help you with your business and whatever you're trying to develop. There are what is called a high maintenance type of investors who are calling every day wanting to know if you're hard at work or if your focused on what's going on with business and know exactly what the next step or stage is.

And there's the low maintenance type of investors who believe in you and the concept you've developed and who allow you freedom to go out there and make things happen. That's the scenario you want to look for. You don't want somebody who is going to be looking over your shoulder all the time. There's enough stress in business and that's one thing to keep in mind.

In developing any kind of partnerships or any joint venture, you want to make sure that you know these people very well. You should look for a partner who has a skill that you don't have. Maybe the partner has a specialty in selling or perhaps it's in marketing or maybe it's just running the day-to-day operation of the business. But think of taking on a business partner in the same way that you think about getting married. When looking at a partnership in business, you're looking at it as lifetime commitment because you want that business be around hopefully forever. But just as in a marriage, many business partnerships have major issues where the two parties can't get along. Often-times that could lead to ruining your business.. You want to make sure you hand-select your partner; get to know him [or her.] Find out everything about your new partner, his or her personal life, "financial habits." Ask yourself is the person good with money?" Find out what motivates them and where they'd like to be in a few years, that way you can determine if it's a long and the path as yours. Don't just settle because you just need somebody to come in and work for you in your business idea. Find somebody that's the perfect match that can compliment you and take advantage of an area that you're not strong in so that you can focus on the areas where you are strong.

The next thing you want to take a look at is the documentation that you have in your business. Are you properly incorporated in the state were you set up your business structure? Did you get the licenses required within that particular state?

Take a look at all your paperwork, including the contracts you have to sign. For example, if you're going to rent some space in a building you'll be signing a lease. You want to know what you and your business are responsible for paying for such as taxes, heat, and electricity, and what your landlord pays for such as overall insurance, cleaning, and maintenance of the common areas of the building. If you aren't fully familiar with contacts or leases, hire the services of an attorney. Allow the attorney to read your leases and your contracts and anything requiring your signature. It is *very* important to protect yourself.

Oral agreements or handshakes are fine, but aren't safe for business. Saying, "I'd like doing business on a handshake," could be the most dangerous area of your business. People have selective memory. They forget exactly what was said at one point or another and it also upsets them when different recollections clash. When it's on paper and it's all laid out, everybody can understand what exactly the intent was, how the contracts were designed, and how they were agreed upon.

Next, you want to take a look at the business structure itself. What business structure is right for you and what are you trying to develop? Becoming incorporated, which I will discuss in greater detail on the next module in this series, has some wonderful advantages. It allows you to raise capital very efficiently. It also allows you to pay taxes that are reduced rate and they protect your assets, one of the most important things in business today.

There also some different types of business structures that we'll take a look at— sole proprietorships, limited partnerships, limited liability companies, the list goes on. One of the most common types of business structures is the sole proprietorship. Sole proprietorship is the place most businesses start. You get a business license in the county you are operating in. Set up your bank account and you're off and running. The benefit of a sole proprietorship is that it's very simple to set up and form. You pay the taxes on your personal income tax return so there is no other tax filing that is required. However, one of the worst parts about sole proprietorship is that all the liability on the business rests on your shoulders. If you get involved in any kind of litigation, everything you have in your business is exposed. Business structures that limit the amount of liability you have make a lot of sense.

The next type of business structure we want to look at is a general partnership. A general partnership is an agreement between two parties who have come together and decided to start an idea. Generally there's an agreement they form that says one person is going to do one aspect of the business and the other person is going to cover another area. You lay out what some of those responsibilities are, along with what compensation to the parties will be. Now, again, just like a sole proprietorship, there are some simple structures to start up and, just like the sole proprietorship, one of the weakest elements of the general partnership is that all liability rests on you as one of the people who run the business. Again, you want to explore business structures that help you limit your exposure and liability.

One of the business structures that is used for investment purposes in Real Estate, stock market, and raising funds for special projects is called a limited partnership. Limited partnerships can be used for business purposes and are heavily used right now for escape planning.

Finally, another type of business structure is called limited-liability company (LLC). This structure limits your liability and it's easy to form and operate.

Don't worry if a lot of this seems overwhelming at first. Remember, there is nobody looking over your shoulder. There's no test at the end. Feel free to stop and make notes and then continue as often as you need to.

Being in business is actually very simple, it amounts to just seeing what is needed and providing it. Whether your business is about products, services, or both, you're providing a solution to a problem that a lot of people want the solution for.

For example, information products give people "how-to" instructions: Truck drivers provide a solution for "how to get products from one place to another." Teachers provide a solution for "how to educate our children." It's the same in every industry; find the problem and offer people a valuable solution at a reasonable price. Of course, getting your initial ideas, business plans, and financing is an important step. But you should also give some thought to how you will keep your business going once you've made it to the initial first phase.

Something else that makes good business practice but which few business owners do is to methodically build a good credit rating with a local bank. Particularly when you have a good cash flow, you should borrow even small amounts of money that you can easily pay back. By doing this, you will increase the borrowing power of your signature and strengthen your ability to obtain needed financing in short notice. This is a kind of business leverage that will be of great value in the future when needed.

You should join your industry's local and national trade associations. Most of these organizations have a wealth of information available, everything from details of your competitors to average industry sales figures to new products, services, and trends.

Whenever you can, and as often as you need it, you should take advantage of whatever free business counseling is available. The Small Business Administration has many excellent booklets, checklists, and brochures available on quite a large variety of businesses. They also have management and financial assistance programs that can definitely benefit just about any small business. Most local universities and many private organizations hold seminars at very minimal cost, often without charge. You should take advantage of free services offered by your bank and local library. Keeping track of your business's finances is important. After all, if you are going to be in business you've got to know how to "keep score."

You don't need to be an accountant yourself; many popular programs out there such as Quicken. They can help you understand the basics of accounting. Having a real accountant, even if the person is someone who just double-checks your numbers, is important for many reasons. Your accountant can help you prepare a cash flow control statement that will estimate what the cash needs of the business will be in the month to come. Your accountant can also help you prepare a personal financial statement, including a balance sheet, of your personal assets and liabilities along with the statement of income and expenses showing how much cash flow you generate each month. Banks will usually require a personal guarantee. He or she can also help as a source of introduction to a banker. This can be helpful because a banker has had prior dealings with the accountant; your accountants can help you put your business plan together for your banker or other financial sources. The accountant organizes as much information as possible, including financial statements, in a neat, orderly fashion. The accountant organizes as much information as possible, including financial statements in a neat, orderly fashion.

There will be a number of tax liability matters that you and your accountant will need to deal with. This includes income taxes. If you start as a sole proprietor, you'll be reporting your business activity to on an IRS form 1040, Schedule C. Not only will the sole proprietor pay income tax on business income but the sole proprietor will also pay Social Security tax on this income. This is reported as a separate item on the income tax return. The Social Security tax can be quite a surprise to the new small businessperson who does not expect to pay roughly 15 percent of net income for Social Security tax on top of his or her income tax.

Operating as a partnership or LLC does not relieve a partner of the obligation of paying self-employment tax. Your accountant can help set up estimated tax payments that will lessen the burden of your final tax bills as well as avoid penalties for not paying taxes as you go along.

Regarding payroll taxes, if you have employees, your account can help you apply for the necessary state and federal payroll numbers you'll need to file payroll tax returns. The federal number is called The Federal Employer Identification Number or FEIN. And this can be obtained using Form FF4.

In every state, there are local and state taxes that are required. For instance, in California, you need to apply for a State Identification Number that will establish an account for you to pay the State Withholding Tax as well as the State Disability Insurance. There's also a State Employment Tax that you pay. There may be some other taxes that are unique to your local situation.

The important thing about running a small business is to know the direction in which you are heading, to know on a day-to-day basis your progress in that direction, to be aware of what your competitors are doing, industry trends and sales figures for businesses comparable to the size of yours.

Practice good money management at all times, and to prepare yourself to solve your problems before they arrive.

So What?

Let's go over some of the ideas we've talked about on this module. What we've seen of the past sixty years of business is that the world continues to change faster and faster each year. Entire industries are replaced by new technologies. People who don't pay attention to this are left lying on the side of the road wondering what they'll ever do for work again. Let's face it, job security doesn't exist anymore.

Take farming for example. Family farms are extinct now and corporations with smart machines have taken over. If you've been farming for thirty years and you can't afford to farm anymore because of factory farms that have taken over the industry, what are you going to do? Farming is a valuable skill but it'll only works for farming. If you are an unemployed farmer and you are adaptable, you can look for an opportunity. You can find a problem that needs to be solved, provide a solution for it, figure out if the numbers are profitable, and if they are create a successful business.

Becoming a business owner and running a successful business can be the most gratifying areas of life. Built on the idea you've always dreamed about requires some risk-taking but do it in a careful and calculated manner. Plan things out properly; make sure that you have enough money set aside. Don't quit your day job prematurely. Spend time developing your ideas and you'll find that being an entrepreneur can be very rewarding. The rewards, both financial and those that come with being independent, are huge. Is there risk involved in being an entrepreneur? Yes. But the rewards far outweigh the stress, as they come in the day-to-day management of the business. Start today by looking at the opportunities that are all around you. Identify your dream, then take the necessary steps to reach your goal.

LIFE IS RICH

"THERE ARE NO "GREY AREAS" WHEN YOU ARE PROFESSIONAL SALESPERSON, NETWORK-MARKETER OR BUSINESS OWNER. NEVER SKATE AROUND THE TRUTH. NO LYING!

WWW.ASKNATESCOTT.COM
904.838.2623

IF YOU WOULD LIE TO GET AN APPOINTMENT OR MAKE A SALE THEN YOU HAVE NO INTEGRITY. IF YOU DON'T HAVE ANY INTEGRITY YOU HAVE NO VALUES. IF YOU HAVE NO VALUES YOU HAVE NO CHARACTER.

AND IF YOU HAVE NO CHARACTER, THEN WHY WOULD ANYONE WANT TO ENTER INTO A RELATIONSHIP WITH YOU AND BUY FROM YOU?

NO LYING!
AM I CLEAR?"

CHAPTER 5
Creating the Right Business Entity

2 Timothy 3:14-17 *"14 But continue thou in the things which thou hast learned and hast been assured of, knowing of whom thou hast learned them; 15 And that from a child thou hast known the holy scriptures, which are able to make thee wise unto salvation through faith which is in Christ Jesus. 16 All scripture is given by inspiration of God, and is profitable for doctrine, for reproof, for correction, for instruction in righteousness: 17 That the man of God may be perfect, thoroughly furnished unto all good works."*

This chapter will show you many other ways of structuring your business other than just by being a sole proprietor. It will talk about what your business entity should be. Should you incorporate? What are the benefits of incorporation? How can incorporation help you? Where should your business be incorporated? Are there any business entities that you should use? What paperwork is necessary to make your business a success? And is this worth it? All of this and more will be covered in this chapter.

There are many ways that your business can be structured. In other words, how can it be legally put together? There will also be myths and misconceptions behind "how can a company become a corporation?" We will discuss all of this in a moment. Let's first look at the easiest form of the business called the Sole Proprietorship.

A Sole Proprietorship is one person working alone. You will have unlimited liability for all debts of the business. In other words, if your company goes under then you are the one person who is responsible. In a Sole Proprietorship, the income or loss from the business will be reported on the business owner's personal income tax return, along with all the other income and expense the business owner normally reports. Many entrepreneurs start their businesses this way, not because of the advantages of being a sole owner, but because they are not familiar with other ways of structuring the business. This module will show you many other ways of structuring your business other than just by being a sole proprietor.

Another possible way of forming your business is that of a General Partnership. In the General Partnership, each of the two or more partners will have a limited liability for the debts of the business. The income and expenses are reported on a separate return for tax purposes, but each partner then reports his portion share of the profit or loss from the business as one line in his personal tax return. With a limited partnership, each of the partners has unlimited liability for the debts of the partnership. But the limited partner's exposure to the debts of the partnership is limited to the contribution each has made to the partnership. With certain minor exceptions, the reporting for tax purposes is the same as for a general partnership. The major way of structuring a business is through incorporation.

Let's examine a little more closely the ins and outs of setting up your business as a corporation.

A corporation provides limited liability for the investors, except in some cases that I'll talk about soon. None of the shareholders in the corporation is obligated for the debts of the corporation.

Unlike the sole proprietorship I talked about a few minutes ago, creditors can look only to the corporation's assets for payment. The corporation files its own tax return, and pays taxes on its income. In addition, a corporation has many tax benefits such as deducting health insurance premiums. A corporation that has elected to be an S Corporation for federal income tax purposes, is treated as a partnership for tax purposes although it is treated as a regular corporation for other purposes.

You don't need to have a large business to be a corporation. In fact, most of the new corporations that are formed each month are small operations. Even the owners of a home-based business may find that incorporating brings them many advantages. In this section, we will discuss the characteristics, advantages, and disadvantages of conducting your business as a corporation.

Corporations are important in business because they help companies raise capital for funding and developing new areas of their businesses. They also are very important when it comes to asset protection or liability protection.

Corporations protect individuals who operate companies or people who just want to invest in a business idea let somebody else come operate the company. They protect them from personal liability in the day-to-day affairs of those companies.

What is a corporation?

A corporation, a non-human entity, is a legal thing apart from you. Corporations exist because of the statute known as the Business Corporation Act (BCA).

The most important feature of a corporation is that it exists entirely separate and apart from its owners. Virtually all of its legal matters and the taxes associated with a corporation flow from its essential element. Once the proper forms are filled out, it's as though a new individual is being created. That individual has some rights, just as you and I do. It can bank, transact any kind of business, get involved in litigation, and use the court systems. The corporation can pretty much do what we do on a day-to-day basis in business. You've created something that is absolutely separate from yourself. Even if you're the only owner and the only employee of the company, your company and you are two separate legal entities. You might be the only one working day-to-day and you might be the only one who ever puts money into the company.

The most important thing to remember is that your corporation is a legal structure that is separate from you and you're the one who operates that business. That corporation can almost be thought of as another person you operate through. You get a tax identification number for that company. You are no longer operating under yourself with your name and you're no longer utilizing your Social Security number for the work of your business day in and day out. The corporation can set up its bank account, get credit cards, and borrow from a bank. Your company can sign leases, purchase Real Estate and other assets, and do all sorts of things through this legal structure so that you as an individual can have some privacy. You're not the one signing the documentation—you're signing on behalf of the corporation.

The corporation's name is the owner of the assets that you purchased or leases that you sign or the name of the bank account itself. It allows you to have privacy and it also protects you from liability and risks in business which I will talk about in a moment.

First, let's talk about some of the tax advantages of having a corporation. If you have a small business, you should consider incorporating to take advantage of favorable tax loopholes. Many people are under the mistaken idea that corporate tax laws are only for the benefit of large corporations. This is not true.

For example, a tax advantage available for your small business corporation, no matter how big or small, is to set up a company medical plan. Health-related expenses are consistently on the rise and are often paid with after tax dollars. The United States has two separate tax systems—employee and business owner. The employee earns, then is taxed, then spends what's left over. The business owner earns, then spends, then is taxed on what's left over.

You pay for health care costs with the remaining money. If you have a corporation, you can set up a company medical insurance and medical reimbursement plan. Your corporation can purchase a group medical insurance plan for your shareholder-employees that will probably include your spouse. Your corporation can also pay for the cost of deductibles, co-payments, and other health-related expenses that are not covered by most health plans. These costs are deductible to the corporation and not considered taxable income to you. The net effect will be to use free tax dollars rather than after tax dollars for your health related expenses.

A question entrepreneurs often ask when incorporating is, "Where do I incorporate?" Nevada and Delaware has favorable corporate laws that limit the liability of directors. As you may know, corporate directors are often sued for breach of fiduciary duty.

Since the laws applied in the case of a lawsuit involving the internal workings of the corporation in a state of formation, Delaware and Nevada offer maximum protection from director liability. Nevada is a particularly favorable jurisdiction because it has no personal or corporate state income tax. Shareholders' privacy is protected in Nevada because there are no corporate state income tax returns filed and no information sharing with the IRS. In addition, there are no franchise taxes, no record of stockholders, no need to live in Nevada, no need to be a United States citizen, and no need for annual meetings in Nevada. Because of affordable incorporation fees and nominal annual renewal fees, one person can fill all offices of the company.

Another example is that Nevada allows bearer shares for its companies. What are "bearer shares"? Simply, bearer shares represent ownership of a corporation just as any other common share of corporate stock has, with one special attribute: they do not identify the shareholder. The owner of the shares is that person or entity who holds the share at that point in time.

Today, in all states except Nevada, the stockholders must be issued a stock certificate reflecting full identification of the stockholder. Nevada is the only remaining state that still allows bearer shares. Bearer shares are like paper dollars owned by the person whose pocket they are in as of today. Those who possess the shares own and control the corporation. Bearer shares are a great tool to restrict information against predatory creditors. (I will talk more about the dangers of these people in just a few minutes.)

"Another common question is, "What entity to choose, S or C status for your corporation?" There are two primary types of corporations for tax purposes: C and S corporations. A C corporation files a tax return and pays taxes on its profits. The C corporation then distributes dividends to its shareholders who claim it as income on their personal tax return. Most large corporations like IBM and Microsoft are C corporations.

An S corporation's profits are not subject to double taxation. A corporation files an informational return and uses IRS Form K1. This form is sent to shareholders, and shows the shareholders' share of income or loss. This income or loss is then reported on the shareholders' personal income tax returns. There's no double taxation but all profits and losses are subject to income tax on the shareholder's returns whether or not the profit is actually distributed or reinvested in the business.

A loss, however, flows through so that the shareholder can use it to offset other income earned. A loss from the C corporation does not flow through but it can be carried forward for future years to offset income or by the corporation.

The S status must be elected. A corporation is a C corporation by default. The C corporation offers certain fringe benefits not available in S corporation.

For example, a C corporation can set up a medical reimbursement and a medical insurance plan for its shareholder-employees. A C corporation can also pay for the group life insurance up to $50,000 in death benefits for its shareholder-employees. Again, this is 100 percent deductible to the corporation and not income to the employees. Finally, a C corporation can offer a profit-sharing plan to its employees that permits the shareholder-employees to borrow money from the plan. The bottom line is that a C corporation is not necessarily better or worse than an S corporation; but rather, it depends on how it's used and the personal tax of the shareholders.

Whether you to choose to structure your business as a C or an S corporation, incorporating has many benefits. These include protection from personal liability. As many of you may know, incorporating is one of the best ways to protect business owners from personal liability. Shareholders of a corporation are generally not liable for the obligations of the corporation. Creditors of the corporation may seek payments from the assets of a corporation but not the assets of the shareholders. This means that the business owners may engage in business without risking their homes and other personal property.

Self-employment tax savings. Corporate profits are not subject to Social Security, medical care, workers compensation, and other taxes, a combined 15.3 percent in taxes. An individual proprietor would need to pay all of these taxes, commonly referred to as self-employment taxes, on all income earned by the business. With a corporation, only salaries are subject to these taxes.

For example, if the sole proprietor earns $60,000 in his or her business, a 15.3 percent tax would need to be paid on $60,000. Let's say that Sam, the owner of a corporation, pays himself $40,000 a year in salary and $20,000 is left over as a corporate profit. In this case, the 15.3 percent tax would only be paid on the salary $40,000. This saves the owner of the corporation more than $3,000 a year. Please note that a stockholder-employee must pay himself or herself a reasonable salary or else the IRS could re-characterize some or all of the corporate profit as salary.

There is a 15 percent tax on corporate profit. C corporations provide even greater tax flexibility by simply dividing income between the corporations and the shareholders. Doing this, businesses can save thousands of dollars each year on taxes.

With a C corporation, the first $50,000 received as dividends is taxed only at 15 percent, and Social Security and Medicare taxes are not withheld. If you incorporate in a tax-free state such as Nevada or Delaware, there is no state income tax. Therefore, if you are in a 28 percent tax bracket and put $50,000 of your personal income into a corporation, you could save about $14,000 per year. This amount includes the money saved by not paying Social Security and Medicare taxes.

How do you avoid the double taxation associated with a C corporation? Never distribute dividends directly to the shareholders or simply pay out dividends in the form of a bonus. Since most corporations are not limited to any particular business activity, corporate profit can be reinvested into other business ventures. Corporate profits can also be spent on employee perks.

Ability to deduct business operating losses. Corporations have very few restrictions on operating and capital losses. Losses are generally carried back for years and can be carried forward for fifteen years. Sole proprietorships not only have more strict rules, but are also subject to a higher probability of getting audited if there are losses.

Fringe benefits, Medical Insurance, and Retirement. Retirement plans such as a 401(k) can be set up by a corporation that could allow you to exclude a higher amount of income than a regular IRA. With a corporate entity, savings may have doubled with a corporate matching program.

Medical Insurance. Corporations can deduct 100 percent of the insurance premiums paid on behalf of the owner-employee. As a sole proprietor filing an individual return, only 60 percent of the medical premium is currently deductible.

Fringe Benefits and Deductions. With proper structuring, a corporation may deduct the other expenses such as automobile insurance, education benefits, and life insurance. These expenses are subject to strict limitations for the sole proprietor, if deductible at all. Moreover, this expense can be a red flag that triggers audits for individuals. For example, an individual proprietor who wants to deduct expenses from a home office can trigger IRS scrutiny.

Lower chance of an IRS audit. On a percentage basis, the IRS conducts fewer audits on corporations than individuals. Corporate returns also raise fewer red flags than individual returns.

One of the risks that a corporation often faces, but seldom wants to talk about, comes from business failure. If you are operating as a sole proprietor and your business fails, you are in potential risk of losing your house. Any personal assets such as your bank account or any stocks or bonds or investments that you might have are at risk. If you operate in a corporate structure and design the paperwork properly, you're not so personally exposed that your business fails or goes under.

Let's now explore a little more deeply how you put together a corporation. Corporations must have at least one owner. But there is no upper limit as to how many people can be owners. The owners are called shareholders or stockholders. The ownership interests of the shareholders of the corporation are divided into units called stocks, shares, or shares of stock. The rules governing corporations, along with the advantage and disadvantages, apply equally to corporations owned by one or more than one shareholder.

A corporation comes into existence when the perspective shareholders file a paper with the State of Authority known as Articles of Incorporation. Among other things, the Article of Incorporation requires the prospective shareholders to determine the number of shares that the corporation will be authorized to issue. The total number of shares the corporation may issue is up to you and there is no upper limit. However, the corporation must issue at least one share of stock for each shareholder. If the corporation will have more than one shareholder, the corporation should issue shares to each shareholder in proportion to their ownership interest.

The proportion of the shareholders' ownership interest may be vary from a fraction of 1 percent to a fraction of more than 99 percent, depending on the deal the shareholders make when they decide to go into business together.

For example, if you're the sole shareholder, it makes no difference if you own one share or one million shares. In each case, you own 100 percent of the corporation. Likewise, if two people decided to go into a business on a sixty–forty basis, it makes no difference if one owns six shares or sixty million and the other one owns four or forty million. In each case, their shares are sixty–forty.

The stockholders' role is to sit back and hopefully reap the reward and the financial success of the company. Typically, they're not involved in the day-to-day operation. They don't make a lot of decisions for the company itself. The shareholders are just there to put the money in and to own the company. The shareholders are the ones who invest or are the owners of the company.

Now let's look at how a corporation does its business. A corporation conducts business through a chain of what we could think of as "proxy people." They are authorized representatives of the shareholders. The shareholders are at the top of the organization's flow chart. They do not directly manage the corporation's daily affairs. Instead, shareholders meet at least once a year to elect a board of directors.

Corporations must have at least one director but there is no limitation as to how many they can have. The director's job is to make general business decisions for the corporation. Their decisions are then implemented by the corporation's officers who are appointed by the directors each year at the directors' meeting. In a small corporation, it is usually just yourself or you and your business partner or spouse, and the two of you become the elected board.

The board of directors must meet at least once a year. In a larger company, sometimes they meet quarterly or in some companies they meet once a month to talk about the direction of the organization. The board of the directors sets the policy and the direction of the company and carries forth the shareholders' wishes. They decide what the corporation is going to do, what its purpose is going to be, who is going to be hired to run and mange the corporation, and major contracts. They decide if they are going to raise capital or bring in money for the organization. The board is there to oversee major policy issues of the company. Every year, the board gets together and reviews the finances of the company. They measure its success, the factors involved, and whether to pursue the current direction. If it's not doing well, they decide the major changes needed to alter the course of the company or maybe get rid of some of the management team they've selected and bring in some fresh people to run and develop it. Again, in a smaller organization, you're the board directors of your own company.

When the board meets once year, it has some responsibilities other than deciding where the company is going and what its role is. It decides on the officers and votes on those officers. The officers of the corporations are really the ones who run and manage the corporation on a day-to-day basis. The officers must consist of at least the following: president, treasurer, and secretary.

The president is responsible for managing the corporation's daily operations. The treasurer manages the corporation's money, while the secretary maintains the corporation's non-financial books and records.

Corporations may also have one or more vice president. A vice president's job may vary depending on the corporation's needs. For example, the corporation may have vice presidents for sales, marketing, operations, personnel, and so on. Let's look at the secretary's role for a minute.

The secretary's role is not the traditional secretary as most people think of; but rather, is the person in charge of the corporate records. This includes managing the corporate record book, looking after the corporate seal, and all the documents of the corporation. The responsibility of managing this paperwork is that of the secretary.

The secretary's job is to make sure that records are complete and kept up to date. It's important that any significant contracts, leases, and documents are properly recorded and easy to understand. Remember, this is a separate legal entity and every time that you do significant business you want to make sure to put the paperwork safely away in the corporate record book. If anybody in the future wishes to go through your corporate record book, they can understand the development of the company, where it's gone, and how it evolves. In a small company, you might be filling in all of these positions. You might be the president, the secretary, and the treasurer of the entire operation.

Let's look at some of this paperwork for a moment. The corporate charter is given to the business owner by the state. It has the state seal on it and the name of the corporation on the front of the document. It documents the day the corporation first filed with the state and it's now your corporation in good standing. So you're up and running.

The documents that are originally filed are called the Articles of Incorporation. This describes the name and address of the company. It describes how many shares of stock the corporation is going to have and describes the foundation of the company. It tells who the first director is going to be and who has filed the paperwork. It also contains information about how long the corporation is going to be in existence, which can be one set time or forever in perpetuity.

In the articles, the liability aspects of the company are laid out. The articles list the names of the directors, the officers, and the people who are involved in running the corporation on a day-to-day basis. It ensures that all the parties involved don't have personal liability for the direction of the business.

The Articles of Incorporation form the first set of records in getting the company off the ground. They are sent to the state and then the state returns a copy to you along with your original charter and that allows you to develop and get your corporation going.

The next major section of the corporation is the by-laws. A document that can be many pages long, it's full of information about how to develop your company. It describes the annual meeting, how simple they are, how often they must be held, and how to inform your people if you've got other individuals who are involved as investors or are board members of your own company. It describes how the process works. Then it describes the directors' responsibilities and how the directors oversee the direction of the company. It talks about the officers, their roles and responsibilities, and the role and responsibilities of the president, secretary, and treasurer as well as how they interact.

When it's time to make a decision, such as opening a bank account or applying for a company credit card, all you do is create a corporation resolution. The resolution instructs the individuals involved in handling the paperwork.

For instance, it will state that the board of directors had a meeting and decided that the president of the company (even if that is you) instructed you to go to the bank and set up a bank account. The documentation goes into a section that inserts "minutes and resolutions" right into your own record book. The company's by-laws are rules on its day-to-day operations.

One last thing, the shareholders may elect themselves as directors. In their capacity as directors, they may then appoint themselves as one or more officers. If you are a sole shareholder, you may elect yourself as the sole director, and as a sole director, you may appoint yourself as president, treasurer, and secretary.

So why go through all of this paperwork? What are the advantages of corporations? The essential element of a corporation is that its existence is entirely separate and apart from the shareholders. This feature gives rise to the principle advantage of corporations.

Liability protection. Because a corporation exists apart from the shareholders, the corporation alone is liable for its debts. Even though they own and manage the corporation, the shareholders are not personally liable for its debts.

For example, let's suppose that I am the sole shareholder of Easy Paving Incorporated, a corporation through which I can conduct my paving business. While attempting to pave my customer's driveway, I accidentally run over some prize rose bushes. The corporation alone is responsible for the damages caused by the action—in this case, the destruction of some valuable flowers. I'm not personally liable. This means that my customer can only reach into the corporation's assets to pay for the damages. All of my personal assets, such as my house, my car, and my savings are protected from my customer's claim. The result might be different if I intentionally damaged my customer's rose bushes or if my corporation has no equipment, bank account, receivables, insurance, or any other assets. Then I might be personally liable. I might also be personally liable if I do not conduct annual shareholders' and directors' meetings and if I do not keep my corporation's property, such as its bank account, separate from my own. Then it might be determined that my corporation is not a real company at all, that it's a sham corporation and that I am personally liable.

In addition to limited liability protection, a corporation offers two tax advantages. First, under the present tax code, a corporation may claim a 100 percent deduction for health insurance that it purchases for the shareholders benefit. Second, a corporation may deduct the cost of life insurance it purchases for its shareholders up to $50,000 per policy.

But there are a few disadvantages of a corporation that you should be aware of. Because a corporation has its own existence, it pays taxes on its own income. However, if corporation has losses, only the corporation and not the shareholders can claim those losses as tax deduction.

Most businesses lose some money at some time or another. This often happens in the startup phase where cash is the tightest. If you're conducting your business through a corporation, you will be unable to deduct business losses until the corporation makes a profit, even if you have personal income from other sources. This delay can be particularly painful for new business owners with limited resources.

After your corporation becomes profitable, you will face another disadvantage, double tax. Double tax occurs when you and your corporation pay tax twice on the same dollar of income. A terrible fate indeed! Double tax can best be explained by an example.

Let's return to the example of Easy Paving Inc. Easy paving and I must both pay taxes based on the income we earned during the calendar year because Easy Paving has its own existence separate from mine. All the income of the business is charged to Easy Paving, not to me. So in any year, Easy Paving pays taxes on the money it makes. If it chooses to give me money as a dividend, I pay taxes on the money I received from that dividend. So, Easy Paving pays taxes and I pay taxes. That's twice with the same money. That's why it is called double taxation.

Double taxation can also occur if you decide to sell your business. If a buyer purchases it, the corporation's assets and the profits from the sale may be subject to double tax. First, your corporation may pay tax on the gain. Second, you may pay taxes on the money when you take it out of a corporation.

Double taxation on income can be avoided to some extent through a mechanism called Zeroing Out. In the example I've talked about, if I've paid myself the bonus on December 31 rather than on January 1, Easy Paving might have deducted the $5,000 payment as business expense. Easy Paving would then have earned and paid taxes of only $5,000 thus avoiding double tax on the $5,000 paid to me.

Zeroing out has its limits. The Internal Revenue Service may not allow deduction for compensation that is deemed to be excessive. Leaving an excessive amount of money in your corporation can also lead into tax problems. These situations generally do not arise unless you are earning a six-figure salary and unless you've accumulated above six figures in your business. However, they can become a real headache for successful entrepreneurs. Fortunately, the Internal Revenue Service provides some relief in the form of an S corporation.

What is an S Corporation?

The issue of delayed deduction of losses, double tax, excess earnings tax, and excess accumulation of tax has led many business owners to form S corporations.

An S corporation has the same structure and limited liability as in C corporations. However, due to a section of the Internal Revenue code known as Sub-chapter S, the shareholders of the corporations that qualify for Sub-chapter status are able to deduct losses in proportion with and to the extent of their investment in the business. S corporation shareholders are also free from double tax, excess earnings tax, and excess accumulation of tax. This is unlike a C corporation in which income is taxed to the corporation. All the income of S corporation, whether from earnings or sale of assets, is taxed directly to the shareholders in proportion to their ownership interests.

Here's an example. John Doe makes $50,000 in net income and pays about $7,500 in self-employment tax. By forming an S corporation, he can take $25,000 of the profit in salary subject to self-employment tax and $25,000 in dividends, which is not subject to self-employment tax. This assumes, of course, that John can justify to the IRS that he can hire an employee in the marketplace for $25,000 to do the same job.

To become an S corporation, you have to file a form within the first seventy-five days of the operation of your company. Once the company is up and running, you file that form with the IRS and let them know you want to be taxed on your personal tax return.

Of course, S corporations have some disadvantages, too. Unlike the shareholders of C Corporation, shareholders owning more than 2 percent of an S corporation only receive a partial deduction on health insurance purchased for them by the corporation. Also, as the top tax rates are higher for individuals than for corporations, an S corporation's shareholders may pay more income tax than a C corporation's shareholders who leave an excessive amount of money in the corporation.

Whether you choose to operate as a C or as an S corporation, following the proper corporate routine is very, very important. Studies show that most small, closely held corporations would not withstand the challenge of a lawsuit or an IRS audit. You may be asking "why not? I thought a corporation would protect me from liability?"

A corporation will protect you from a liability, but only if you follow the corporate formalities. Use the following as checklist: Did you hold an organization meeting and appoint a board of directors? Did your board of directors appoint officers? Do you have written minutes of these meetings? Do you have a federal tax ID number? Did you physically issue the shares of stocks? Does your corporation have its own bank account? Do you commingle your personal funds with your corporate funds? That is, did you use the corporate checkbook to purchase personal items and vise versa? Does your corporation have a business license, a telephone in its own name, and a physical office address with a written lease? Do you have annual meetings with the shareholders and the board of directors? Do you have written meetings of these meetings? Do you sign all of your leases, contracts, and letters in the capacity in which you are acting, such as the president or secretary?

Your failure to follow one or more of these formalities may result in a "piercing of the corporate veil." This is a legal expression for the process by which the court can actually penetrate the invisible wall of protection between you and your corporation and permit a creditor to go after you personally. If you feel like skipping some of these items because they might take a little bit of time or money, ask yourself whether Microsoft or any large company would violate any of these items.

The lesson here is that if you want to be treated like a legitimate corporation, then act like one. Go and dust off that big black corporate minute book that you tossed in the closet years ago. Look through the forms—the process is not rocket science. It's simply a matter of keeping things in order in case of a lawsuit or an IRS audit. You don't need to run your corporations with rigidity, you simply need a paper trail to justify what you're doing.

Here are a few more tips: If you use your spare bedroom as an office, have written leases between you and your corporation. Make it a net lease so that your corporation can pay you for its share of the utilities, taxes, and insurance on your home. If you constantly funnel money between your personal and corporate bank accounts, draw up the Line of Credit Agreement between you and your corporation. That way, the piecemeal payment that goes back and forth will appear perfectly normal. After all, isn't that what you do with your credit card account?

If you need a legitimate office and phone, consider an executive suite. There are companies that will rent an office address and answering service for as little as $75 a month. This will not only give your corporation legitimacy, but it will give you a place to meet an occasional client as well. Don't wait until you are sued or audited to start filling out the necessary paperwork. An ounce of prevention is worth a pound of regret.

Another part of putting your corporation together is insurance. Insurance as a means of protection should never be overlooked. Insurance will cover many claims such as slip and fall, negligence, etc. The fact that you have insurance to cover this type of claim will help if your corporation is undercapitalized. If you do not have insurance and someone who is injured sues your shell corporation, then the court may think you are not playing fair. This is particularly important if your business is engaged in activities that are dangerous and hazardous to the public.

Another benefit of insurance is that the duty of an insurance company to defend or pay for your legal defense is much broader than its duty to indemnify or pay for the judgment against you. Legal fees alone can be painful, especially for frivolous lawsuits even if you win in court. Here are some available insurance products for your protection.

General Business Liability Insurance. This type of insurance can be reasonable and will cover a wide range of lawsuits from personal injury claims to copyright violations. Obviously, the higher the deductible, the cheaper the insurance. It may be worthwhile to keep an insurance policy with a large deductible and high limits to substitute for having to keep excess capital in your corporation.

Malpractice Insurance. Lawyers, doctors, engineers, architects, Real Estate brokers, and other professionals can obtain Malpractice or Errors and Omissions Insurance. This insurance covers mistakes that you and your employees make in dealing with clients. This insurance can be very expensive depending upon the type of business in which you are involved. In addition, the coverage is weak because the policy covers claims made—it only covers claims made in the year that the policy is in effect. Regular liability insurance will cover you if you are sued years later for events that have occurred during the policy period. In many states, the statute of limitations for malpractice is six years. So, a lawsuit years later will not be covered if you do not maintain continuous coverage.

Director Liability Insurance. Director liability can be so precarious that many people refuse to serve on the board of any corporation without director liability insurance. This insurance is expensive and may not be necessary for a small corporation.

Umbrella Liability Insurance. An umbrella policy is one that kicks in after all underlying policies are exhausted. For example, if you have general liability insurance with $100,000 and a judgment is made against your corporation for $500,000, the umbrella policy kicks in the other $400,000.

Umbrella insurance does not cover other claims that are otherwise not insured, for example a breach of contract claim. Most insurance companies require you to maintain all of your insurance with their company before they will list you on an umbrella policy. Umbrella policies are quite reasonable and can cover your business for up to several million dollars.

Extended Home Owners Insurance. A typical homeowner's policy will cover basic policy claims against you regarding the property. It will not cover general liability claims unrelated to your property. For example, if you injure another person while you are riding your boat on a nearby lake, this claim will not be covered unless your homeowner's policy has a special endorsement.

Review your policies with your insurance agent as to covered issues and policy limits. If cost is an issue, increase your deductible. A lower deductible in a policy is generally more expensive than a higher coverage limit for a liability.

Let's move on to other forms of corporations you should be familiar with. There are two basic forms of corporations. The type we've been talking about so far are: For Profit Corporation, they try to make as much money as possible. Non-profit companies, for example charities, can't have profits. In fact, at the end of the year they have to get rid of all profit made.

There are some benefits of a non-profit company that can be discussed with your accountant or adviser.

There are different types of organizations such as closely held organizations. When we talked about a closely held corporation, we're really talking about what is considered a personal corporation—a company that is used for small business structure. The corner stores or other small businesses are called "closely held," meaning that the shares are being held by people who are close together like family members who are one or two business partners who got together.

There's another designation that we sometimes look at called Personal Service Companies. Personal Service Corporations are corporations that are run for personal services such as a chiropractor or CPA or attorney. These are considered personal services and a different type of corporation because they have a different tax rate they pay as a personal service corporation.

The opposite of closely held companies are public companies. Private means the shares and stocks are held by private investors. Public means its stock is available to the public to be purchased and sold. For instance, you might see a company listed on the New York Stock Exchange (NYSE) or National Association of Securities Dealers Automated Quotations (NASDAQ). These are publicly traded companies. Before I wrap up the subject of how to start up your company, there is more paperwork involved.

Taking care of the legal issues associated with starting up a new business will keep you out of hot water in the future. Here are the first steps you need to take no matter what form your company takes:

1. *Register your business name if you don't incorporate.* Your business name must be registered if it is something other than your full legal name. This is a way of informing the public that you will be doing business as (d.b.a.) and have assumed a fictitious name. Generally, a search is done to insure your name is not already in use and an application is submitted to make it official. Some states require a notice be published in a local newspaper. The details of registering vary from state to state, so check with your state office or county clerk for specifics.

2. *License your business.* Licensing of your business will depend on the type of business you plan to start. Licensing occurs on the state and or local level. Federal licensing is only necessary for businesses that engage in specifically controlled items. This includes things the sale and/or manufacturing of firearms, alcohol, tobacco products, and so on. Many cities, but not all, require a general business license. There may also be a license required for your particular type of business. You should contact your state and city clerks' offices to find out what licenses you need.

3. *Report Income Tax.* You are responsible for filing and paying income taxes on your business. Assuming your business is a sole proprietorship, you'll pay income tax on your net profits. If you're a corporation, your corporation has to file tax. You report your income tax using form 1040 at tax time with the additional requirement of filing Schedule C or C, E, Z profit or loss from business. You can get IRS publications 334, tax guide for small businesses. For more information, visit the IRS online for publications and detailed filing requirements.

4. *Pay Estimated Taxes.* If you expect to owe more than $1,000 on federal taxes, you need to make estimated payments quarterly. This may feel like a burden at first but it actually protects you from actually paying a big amount at tax time. You can learn about this in IRS publication 505, under Estimated Tax Payments.

5. *Pay Self-Employment Tax if you are not incorporated.* You are required to pay self-employment tax on income of more than $400 using schedule SC. Why? That's your contribution to Social Security and Medicare.

6. *Get a State Sales Tax Certificate.* Contact your state treasury office for information on obtaining a sales tax certificate. This certificate obligates you to pay applicable sales tax on goods you sell. If your product is to be sold wholesale or you're buying materials wholesale, inquire about a resale certificate to avoid paying taxes twice.

7. *Obey zoning regulations.* Be sure to check with your city and county offices of zoning regulations on your office locations. You don't want to be in the position of being shut down because of zoning violations.

8. *Get Free Advice.* The SBA, Small Business Administration, is a good place to learn more about the nuts and bolts of legally operating a small business in your area. This office can answer many if not all of your questions about doing business locally.

So What?

So let's review the benefits of a corporation so you can get a general idea of how it works.

Corporations are legal structures that are set up in the state where you originally organize them. They're separate from you as an individual. They're designed to protect you from the personal liability related to your business. In a world where people are constantly suing each other, as well as being sued, this is important protection to have. It is also a convenient structure for raising capital and having to bring in outside investors. They give you some wonderful tax benefits as well.

For instance, if you're in business today, and you're not incorporated, there is only a percentage of your medical expenses and insurance fees that you can deduct. As a corporation, you can deduct 100 percent of your expenses. There is paperwork associated with pursuing a corporate strategy. Meetings must be held and records kept. But you don't need a team of lawyers and a dozen outsiders to be a board of directors. The paperwork is minimal when you weigh it against the advantages I have discussed. In any case, there is paperwork associated with any business even, if you decide not to incorporate at this time. Keeping the right paperwork associated with the right business structure you choose is a key factor of your wealth creation strategy.

CHAPTER 6
Asset Protection

John 10:10 "*10 The thief cometh not, but for to steal, and to kill, and to destroy: I am come that they might have life, and that they might have it more abundantly.*"

In this chapter I will cover the subject of numerous ways to structure your business and assets to protect what you have. The three things I mention are: Using Limited Partnerships, Using Limited Liability Corporations, and Assets Stripping as a Way of Protecting Yourself.

Don't worry if there are a lot of terms here that are new to you. Remember, you can read this section as often as you wish whenever the time is convenient for you. Nobody is grading you and you can learn different things from this chapter at different times in your business life.

For example, if you're just starting a business today, you'll be most interested in understanding the business structure of limited partnerships and limited liability corporations. When, later on, you have accumulated a significant amount of assets as a result of what you have learned, you may become more interested in "assets stripping" techniques. We've got a lot to cover, so let's get started.

In the previous chapters I've talked about the various forms that your business can take, including being a sole proprietor and the benefits of incorporation. If you're operating with a business partner, you may want to consider the benefits of operating as a limited partnership.

A limited partnership is the partnership that has at least one limited partner and one general partner. Most states require filing the certificate with the state in order to be recognized as a limited partnership.

The limited partners generally have no liability beyond their contribution to the partnership. If the limited partnership business fails, the creditors cannot go after the limited partner for that. Furthermore, limited partners are not personally liable for wrongful acts committed by the other partners. In exchange for this limited liability, the limited partners give up their right to participate in the control and management of the partnership.

The general partners run the management of the partnership. The general partners look after the business and control the cash distributions to the partners. The general partners also have unlimited liability as is the case of the general partnership.

Creditors of the partnership can look to the general partner's personal assets, if the limited partnership's assets are insufficient in meeting all the debts that have been undertaken. Furthermore, the general partners are liable to the third parties for wrongful conduct within the partnership business such as the "slip and fall" lawsuit and the full-range lawsuits.

The limited partnership does not have to pay taxes as a business; instead, it files an informational tax return to the IRS. It uses a Form K1, sent to the partners to include the partnership income or loss on their personal tax returns. The partners must file their income tax on all gains, whether or not profit is distributed to them. Creditors of individual partners cannot take a partner's place in the partnership.

A creditor may garnish the partner's share of income called a Charging Order but has no right to participate in the management or utilize partnership property. Thus, if the limited partner's income is garnished by a creditor, then the general partner who should be under the limited partner's control can frustrate the creditor by not distributing income to the partners. Since the partners are required to pay taxes on his or her share of income whether or not income is distributed, guess who pays the tax bill? You guessed it, the creditor. The result is that if your assets are held by a limited partnership, they are virtually judgment proof.

Now let's look at the variation of this called a Family Limited Partnership. Suppose that you and your spouse create a limited partnership to hold your family's liquid assets, your limited partnership contributions are all of your stocks, cash, CDs (certificates of deposit), and mutual fund totaling $500,000. Your partnership agreement could state that your spouse will act as a general partner with a 2 percent share. The size of a general partnership does not affect the general partner's power to manage the partnership affairs. You'd have something in writing stating that the contribution cost was for 98 percent limited partnership interest. The partnership agreement could further state that the limited partnership shall have the right to buy out the general partner for his or her share of partnership and appoint a new general partner to replace him or her. This is the business structure that you have set up.

Now, let's say that you are sued and the creditor has obtained $100,000 judgments against your name. The creditor can attach your limited partnership interest but only to the extent of your income as a limited partner. The creditors who attach the limited interest cannot participate in the management of the partnership and thus cannot force the general partner—your spouse—to distribute income. As a general partner, your spouse stops paying the limited partner's distributions because, according to his or her discretion, the limited partnership is better served to reinvest the capital rather than pay it out.

One year later, the creditor still has the $100,000 unsatisfied judgment. Remember that no money has been paid out to the creditor. Just to top it off, the partner sends the creditor a Form K1 for the creditor's share of what would have been your income. In our example, the partnership assets are worth $500,000 at a 10 percent annual return. Your share of income will be at least $50,000. So where does this leave us? Well, first remember that no money has been paid out to the creditor. Secondly, the creditor would have to pay income taxes on the income of $50,000. If the creditor does not pay the tax that is due to the distributed income, the IRS could come after the creditor.

All of this leaves you in the strong position of being able to negotiate with any potential creditors if your assets are held by Family Limited Partnership. As you can see, the limited partnership is one of the few entities that give you control of your money but still provide you with the asset you want. This is a powerful tool that you should consider as part of your personal affairs.

Here's another structure of doing business. As of April 1, 1997, all fifty states have adopted Limited Liability Company (LLC) Laws. Basically, the LLC is a cross between a corporation and a partnership with all the bells and whistles of both.

Limited liability companies have been used extensively throughout Europe and South America during the past thirty years. Limited liability companies are the type of partnership where two or more parties have come together to transact some kind of business. This can be any type of business at all, including investing in a project or doing some kind of business deal where a couple of people have decided to pool their resources and try out a new project.

A limited liability company is a very simple business structure that provides limited liability protection for individuals who come together collectively to create some kind of business idea. It is created by state law. It's there to allow you to transact business in a manner where you're not personally liable for the risk and the perils of your business, just like a corporation.

An LLC is a separate and distinct legal entity. This means that an LLC can obtain a tax identification number, open a bank account, and do business all under its own name.

But unlike a normal corporation there is a difference. The primary advantage of an LLC is that its owners, known as members, are not personally liable for the debts and the liabilities of the LLC. For example, if an LLC loses a lawsuit that forced it to declare bankruptcy, the members will not be required to make up the difference with their own money. If the assets of the LLC are not enough to cover the debts and liabilities, the creditors can't look to the members, managers, or officers for additional money. An LLC can be taxed either as a pass through entity like a partnership or sole proprietorship where the money is passed through the members who in turn pay tax, or as a regular corporation.

If an LLC chooses to be taxed as a pass through, and most do, the owners of the LLC are not subject to double taxation. This is as opposed to a regular taxation that requires payment of the corporate tax on its net income—the first tax—and then a second tax when the corporation distributes its profit as stockholders pay taxes on dividends. Partnerships and sole proprietorships do not have to be treated as tax-paying entities. The profit is passed to the owners who pay taxes at their individual tax rate.

Let's take a look now at how an LLC compares to a more typical corporation. What are the advantages of an LLC? The first is that there are fewer corporate formalities. Corporations must hold a regular meeting of the board of directors and shareholders keep written corporate minutes and file annual reports with the state. All of this paperwork I mentioned in the early chapters has to be filled out and submitted regularly. On the other hand, the members and managers of an LLC need not hold regular meetings. That reduces complications and paperwork.

Another advantage of LLCs is that there are no ownership restrictions. An S Corporation is limited to seventy-five stockholders and each stockholder must be a natural person who's a resident or a citizen of the United States. There are no such restrictions placed on an LLC.

A corporation is usually bound to the accrual method of accounting, whereas most Limited Liability Corporations can use the cash method of accounting. This means that income is not earned until it is received, which can be very beneficial in some cases.

Another plus to LLCs is the ability to deduct losses. Members who are active participants in the business of an LLC are able to deduct its operating losses against the members' regular income to the extent permitted by law. Shareholders of an S corporation are also able to deduct operating losses but shareholders of C corporations are not.

Finally, the last advantage comes in an area of employment taxes. A member-employee of an LLC is not required to pay an employment insurance tax on his or her salary. Shareholder-employees of a corporation must pay this tax.

Currently the federal employment tax is 6.2 percent of the first $117,000 of wages paid to a maximum of $7,254 per employee. But along with these advantages is also a disadvantage that you should know about.

First, the profit of an LLC is subject to Social Security and Medicare taxes. In some circumstances, owner-employees of an LLC may end up paying more taxes than owner-employees of a corporation. In some circumstances, owner-employees of an LLC may end up paying more taxes than owner-employees of a corporation. Salary and profits of an LLC are subject to self-employment taxes currently equal to a combined 15.5 percent. With a corporation, only salaries, not profit, are subject to such taxes. This disadvantage is significant to member-employees who take a salary of less than $72,600.

For example, if a member earns $40,000 in salary and his or her dividend is $20,000, a tax of 15.5 percent will have to be paid on the total—$60,000. For an S corporation, Social Security and Medicare taxes will only have to be paid on a salary of $40,000. Be aware that IRS frowns upon employee-owners of an S corporation not paying themselves a reasonable salary and simply receiving profits. In situations where IRS determines that shareholders are taking too little in salary, the IRS will re-characterize all or part of the profit as salary.

Another disadvantage of an LLC is that the owners should immediately recognize profit. A C corporation does not have to immediately distribute its profits to its shareholders as a dividend. This means that shareholders in a C corporation are not always taxed on the corporation's profit. Because an LLC is not subject to a double taxation, the profits of the LLC are automatically included in the member's income.

There are a few fringe benefits on LLCs. A member-employee of an LLC who received a fringe benefit such as group insurance, medical reimbursement plans; medical insurance or parking must treat these benefits as taxable income. The same is true to stockholder-employees who own more than 2 percent of an S Corporation. However, a stockholder-employee of a C corporation who receives fringe benefits does not have to report these benefits as taxable income.

Once you've determined that an LLC is right for you, you should decide where you want to form your LLC. An LLC can now be formed in any of the fifty states. Many people choose to form an LLC in Nevada because of the state's long history of pro-business initiatives. Delaware has also gained popularity to due its pro business environment and lack of formal information sharing in an agreement with the IRS. Neither Delaware nor Nevada has corporate income taxes, and business filings in these states can usually be performed more quickly than in other states.

Many people also choose to form LLCs in their home state. This may save you money because the LLC will not need to register as a formed LLC if it does business in its own state and there is no need to pay another person to serve as a registered agent. If your home state has high annual LLC fees or income taxes and your LLC does not do business in that state, it may be wise to form the LLC elsewhere. "Doing business" means more than just selling products or making passive investments in that state, it usually requires having an office or otherwise having an active business presence.

Once you've decided where to form your LLC, you'll have to think of a name for it. In general, the name of a limited liability company must end with the word LLC, LLC, Limited Liability Company, or LTD Liability Co.

The name of the owner may be used as part of the name of the LLC. If the name of the LLC is used in connection with goods or services, you may wish to consider obtaining federal trademark protection for the name. This will ensure that no one in the United States may use that name in connection with the same general type of goods or services, except in areas where someone else is already using that name.

How is an LLC established? Just as a corporation, some documents are filed with the state where you originally decide to place that Limited Liability Company. You have to keep a record book, which is very similar to that of a corporation. In the record book are documents—Articles of Organization—that show exactly how the LLC was set up. These are vitally important documents.

The Articles of Organization contain the information that was given to the state where the LLC was formed. When you decided to set up that Limited Liability Company, you submitted the Articles of Organization to the state and the state accepted them. Then they send back a charter that says you are "now official" and that you are now a Limited Liability Company in that state.

The Articles of Organization state how the LLC was established. The Articles state the name of the Limited Liability Company, the principal location or where the LLC is operating from and how the owner is going to run his or her company.

For example, are you going to have the owners or the members manage it, or are you going to hire a manager to run and oversee the organization? There are clauses that limit the company's liability, informing the public about how that company was set up and what the liability factors are. If anyone tries to sue your Limited Liability Company, they're going to know specifically what their limitations are by reading the Articles of Organization.

The next set of documents you need to understand is the Operating Agreement. The Operating Agreement is much like the by-laws of a corporation. They are the rules of the company. They're all about how you operate that company on a day-to-day basis. The Operating Agreement states what the members' responsibilities are and how involved they need to be in the organization. It points out that you issued certificates of ownership within the LLC. These are much like stock certificates. A certificate of Ownership represents ownership. If there are one hundred certificates, in your LLC, the certificates might represent 100 percent of the company. If someone owns 20 percent of the certificates that have been issued, it means he or she owns 20 percent of the organization.

The Operating Agreement shows the state how the company is to be run and managed. Your ownership of the LLC might be different from the way that profits are distributed to the members. The one person who is running and building the company might get 80 percent of the profit even though he or she only owns 50 percent of the company. The individual who puts money in the organization and who owns half of the company might only get 20 percent of the profits of the company. In your Operating Agreement will dictate exactly how that is laid out so that there are no misunderstandings between the partners or the parties involved.

The Operating Agreement also lays out what the business can and cannot do. It's a very important document and anytime you think about setting up a Limited Liability Company, you want to think about putting the rules together. The moment more than one person is brought into a business, you must have a strategy to establish responsibilities and clearly outline them. This includes assigning responsibilities.

In any kind of partnership situation, partnerships might not last or work out the way you want them to. Think of the business partnership as a marriage. In a partnership with two individuals who have business ideas to share, what is the likelihood that they will stay together for ten, twenty, or in the worst case scenarios. For instance, what if you decided to get out of the business? What if your partner gets out of the business? What happens if either of you die? Do you have rules about bringing in family members to the business? What about spouses? Are they allowed to work in the business or do you keep them out? All this needs to be put in writing for a successful partnership.

Some of the most successful LLCs are structured where investors have functioned in a similar way as a board of directors. And they hired managers to represent their interest. The actual investors themselves were not involved in the day-to-day-operations.

Now we turn to running your LLC. A Limited Liability Company may be managed either by the members or by one or more managers. A member is an owner of the company. If an LLC is managed by its members, then the owners are directly responsible for running the company.

A manager is a person elected by the members to manage the company. In this context, a manager is similar to a director of a corporation. A manager can be, but is not required to be, a member. If an LLC is managed by managers, then its members are not directly responsible for running the company.

Whether an LLC should be managed by members or managers depends on several factors, including the number of owners, the type of business, where the owners are located, and how involved the members will be in its operations. Management by members is usually the best option for LLCs that have only one member or just a few members, all actively participating in the affairs of the LLC. If there are many members, on the other hand, including some who do not actively participate in the operations of the LLC such as silent partners, then management by managers may be the best option.

Regardless of how a Limited Liability Company is managed, the owners can still appoint officers to run the day-to-day operations of the company. An LLC is not, however, required to have officers. Officers serve at the pleasure either of the manager(s), if the Limited Liability Company is managed by manager(s), or the members, if the Limited Liability Company is member managed.

Members or managers may also be officers. There is no limit on the maximum number of officers neither is there a limit on the members of offices that a person may hold. In fact, the same person may hold all of the offices. Just as with any other corporate structure, keeping the paperwork correct is very important with Limited Liability Companies, even though there is less paperwork generally involved in LLCs than in any other corporate structures I have discussed.

As we mentioned, it's important to keep the business and affairs of the LLC separate from a member's or manager's personal affairs. This means setting up a separate bank account, maintaining separate records, and keeping separate accounts. Regular or annual meetings of the members or managers are not required. Even though it is not required by law, it may be a good idea to take records of the actions taken or approved at meetings.

Transfers of membership interests generally require the consent of the other members of the LLC. This is an important issue to consider for any LLC with more than one member. On one hand you may wish to sell or transfer your membership units to anyone you wish. On the other hand, if you consider the other members of the LLC your business partners, you may want approval of whether they can transfer their interest and to whom they can transfer it.

So, when is it really best to use an LLC? There are certain types of situations where Limited Liability Companies have wonderful attributes. For instance, they are useful if you are involved in buying and selling Real Estate or if you're involved in buying Real Estate such as single family homes or apartment complexes. These Real

Estate deals can produce losses from their depreciation over the first few years that you own and operate it.

The thing to keep in mind is that you want those losses to go directly to you. Often times this is done to offset other income, which they do in an LLC. Owning Real Estate also exposes you to some liability issues that can be avoided in an LLC. What if the water heater breaks in the house you rent out? What if there's led paint on the walls? What if there's asbestos in the basement? You never know what you're getting into with a house. What if somebody falls and trips down the stairs because a piece of carpeting was loose or something else happened? They're going to go after you, the owner of the property. If you hold that piece of Real Estate in a legal structure like a Limited Liability Company, you can be protected. What happens is that outsiders can only sue the business structure; they can't sue you, the owner, because it's in an LLC.

Investments are another area suited for a Limited Liability Company. If you want to invest in a project with a Limited Liability Company, you don't have the same kind of limitations you may have with the corporation where the security regulations are very strict with the number of investors you can actually bring on without having to publicly register your offering your investors.

You can bring in a hundred investors simply with a Limited Liability Company and let them know it will be a simple business structure and any profit is going to flow through to them; your losses will also go directly to them as well. Let's say you have a wonderful new product but it's going to take $10M to produce it and manufacture it and then get it to market. You can bring in a hundred investors simply with a Limited Liability Company and let them know it's will be a simple business structure and any profit is going to flow through to them; your losses will also go directly to them as well.

LLCs are typically not the best structure to hold your passive investments such as stocks or bonds or assets that produce no income at all such as your personal car or a boat you use for recreational purposes. They're really designed to be operating companies, just like corporations are. Their design is to be in a business scenario working day in and day out.

If you and some parties decided to invest in a type of project such as a new software company that somebody created or a new eCommerce business, that's what they are for. You would still use corporations for most business applications, especially where you're the only one who is running and overseeing the operation. The moment you acquire a partner, look at establishing a Limited Liability Company.

It's an opportunity for you to set up a structure where you can decide how the profits and losses are managed because the profits or losses are going to come to you personally.

Let's talk a bit about LLCs and the IRS. They are recognized in all fifty states right now. But as a relatively new business structure, they haven't won any case laws in most states. This is unlike corporations that have been around for hundreds of years in the United States and there are a lot of case laws lying on every type of scenario.

For example, stockholders might sue a president or the directors of the company. Many conservative lawyers and CPAs have in the past shied away from LLCs because it was not clear how the IRS would classify such an entity. However, new IRS rulings make it clear that an LLC will be treated as a partnership as long as it has at least two members.

A single-member LLC will be disregarded for tax purposes. This means that a single member LLC is still valid under state law and thus affords lawsuit protection but no additional tax reporting is necessary at the federal level.

So an LLC, like a corporation, provides lawsuit protection for its owners. The owners, called members, of an LLC are not personally liable for debts or liabilities of the company. Thus an LLC that holds Real Estate will protect its owners from personal liability as a result of lawsuits.

In addition, a foreclosure against the company will not create personal liability for the members unless, of course, the members sign personally on the loan. Like a partnership, the LLC provides pass-through tax treatment. This means that the company is not taxed on its profits. All profits of the company pass through to its members. A regular corporation called the C corporation is taxed at the corporate level. The shareholders are taxed again on the income they received from the company.

Another interesting feature of an LLC is that the IRS does not consider a single-member LLC to exist for tax purposes. Thus, the single member still has lawsuit protection in state court but the member can continue to report his rental income and expenses on schedule E of his personal income tax return.

Here's an example of a simple but effective strategy using this feature. In this example, Larry Landlord does not need to file separate tax return of each of his three LLCs. However, if a tenant in his apartment building is injured, he will not be personally liable neither will he risk losing his other rentals in a lawsuit. As you can see, the LLC can provide excellent protection for landlords with little paperwork hassle.

The LLC can provide a vehicle for passing wealth to younger family members without having to re-title real estate. Once real estate is transferred into an LLC, the members' interest is converted to personal property, which is represented by their LLC shares. These shares can be transferred incrementally to children as tax-free gifts, $10,000 worth per year. The process for transferring LLC shares is very simple compared to filing a new deed each year. The parents can still retain control of the property during their lifetime by acting as managers for the company.

So What?

Before we finish, let's review some of the features of a Limited Liability Corporation. The LLC is a highly general partnership where two or more parties come together as partners in the company. The parties are protected from liability, risks, or pitfalls in businesses today. Taxes are paid by the owners based on the money that flows to owners from the LLC. The LLC itself does not pay taxes to the Internal Revenue Service.

As far as the documentation goes, to create an LLC there are some simple documents that are filed with the state where you decide to set up the business. The documents are then placed in record books to make it very simple to run and manage. There aren't very many requirements, on an annual basis, to keep the company up and running. They're working for you for your benefit. As you can see from this discussion, LLCs can play an important role in your overall asset protection for state planning and tax strategies.

Before we leave the subject of protecting what you have, we should talk more of equity stripping. The basic idea behind this is to own very little in your own name but to control as much as you can.

Equity stripping is perhaps the best technique available to protect real property from creditors. The theory behind equity stripping is that if you don't own interest in the property, the equity is stripped out. There is nothing for a creditor to get; therefore a creditor would not spend time and money to attempt to get that property.

This might be thought of as a high-end technique only used by the wealthy. People have been using equity stripping techniques for a long time. The most common technique is to hold assets in your spouse's name. Here, you simply deed to your spouse your interest in any property. While the advantage here is that it is the cheapest way to structuring your affairs, the disadvantage is that most creditors' attorneys know about this technique and look for it. Another disadvantage of this is that your spouse may divorce you, leaving you with no interest. The court may consider it a fraudulent transfer and just ignore it.

So the easiest way to equity-strip is not really the best. Taking a first or second loan from a bank is the easiest and most common way to equity-strip your property. You now have the cash, which is much easier to protect from creditors than real property. And with the cash invested, it would hopefully draw at a rate higher than your mortgage interest and mortgage costs.

The advantage is that you can get a home mortgage deduction. It is also not likely to be considered a fraudulent transfer if the bank has no notice of any pending claim or judgment against you and no lean has been filed against the property. Of course, the disadvantage is that you essentially surrender control to the bank. If you don't make payments to the bank, keeping in mind that you will probably be denying to a creditor that you are liquid, the bank will foreclose whether or not you desire foreclosure.

In addition, the bank will probably only give you a loan of 80 percent of the equity. Since the bank will be concerned about fluctuations and property value and liquidation costs. So you'll probably leave 20 percent unprotected. If the creditor forces liquidation, you will lose this unprotected equity and any appreciative value. And if your liquid cash, derived from the loan, does not grow faster than your mortgage rate plus costs, then economically you will be a net loser.

Another method of equity-stripping is called Cross Collateralization. This is a technique involving the use of control corporations. Essentially it works this way: Assume you own Corporation A and Corporation B and both corporations own property, you cause Corporation A to take a loan from Corporation B that is secured by Corporation A's property.

You then use the loan proceeds to give a loan back to Corporation B, which gives Corporation A a lien on Corporation B's property. Thus, the property of both Corporation A and Corporation B have had a lien placed on them and are protected from creditors, at least to the extent that the creditors can't figure out or come off with a claim that the transactions were without economic meaning and were fraudulent transfers.

Thus, if Corporation A has a creditor and the creditor has not figured out that Corporation B is part of the same economic family, then Corporation A's property is sold and the proceeds transferred to Corporation B in the satisfaction of the loan, thus, leaving the creditor holding an unenforceable judgment.

While this example is pretty transparent, it would probably be deemed an unacceptable transfer if the creditor figured it out. It illustrates, however, how cross collateralization techniques can operate.

Assume, in this example, that there are three or four corporations. Some of them are off shore and several trusts and private foundations to hold the property, and that the transaction has some real economic substance within the client's business. In such case, it might be very difficult for a creditor to get the complete picture, or to go further to prove that the transactions were without substance and amounted to fraudulent events. However, a Limited Liability Corporation is normally a much better entity to hold a property than any equity-stripping techniques. An LLC gives you asset protection. It flows through any tax losses. There is less paperwork involved than a corporation and certainly less paperwork than equity-stripping techniques that involve forming a number of companies, partnerships, and trusts. All that being said, a Limited Liability Corporation should be in your arsenal of wealth-generating and wealth-keeping strategies.

CHAPTER 7
Financing Your Enterprise

Luke 14:28-30 *"28 For which of you, intending to build a tower, sitteth not down first, and counteth the cost, whether he have sufficient to finish it? 29 Lest haply, after he hath laid the foundation, and is not able to finish it, all that behold it begin to mock him, 30 Saying, This man began to build, and was not able to finish."*

In this chapter, I will talk about finding the money you need to get your business up and running. I will point you to a dozen sources of funding that you may not have thought about. I'll also explore how to build the credit that your company will need throughout its lifetime and the types of business structures that you may want to put in place for yourself and your business.

Entrepreneurs are typically very anxious to get the credit and financing that they will need to get their business up and running. This is a good thing, but just being excited about an idea—and a true entrepreneur can become more excited than almost anybody when it comes to starting his or her business—is not enough. You will need to carefully plan the process of financing your business, and later on get the credit you need.

Your very first step is to create a business plan. If you have a business, you need a business plan. Just the action of creating the plan will help you to think through what you plan to do and why. All of this will help to give your strategies the greatest chance for success. On an ongoing basis, the business plan is what keeps you going in the right direction and gives you a yardstick you can measure your progress by. It quantifies the work that will be involved and functions as a guide for your business development as well. If you are looking to gain any outside funding from lenders or investors, you will need to show them a business plan to demonstrate that your plan is well thought out and holds considerable potential for success. Even if you don't plan on seeking outside money initially to fund your business, it is worthwhile to have a business plan. Think of it as a road map to get where you want to go. The business plan can communicate to others that you will have internal discipline and standards for operating your business successfully. It communicates to government loan agencies, financial institutions, investors, and anyone else interested in the business what you plan to do.

And is a business plan important for finding the funding that you need? It certainly is. According to the U.S. Small Business Administration, all sources for capital will want to see your plan for the start up and growth of your business. If you don't have a business plan, make writing one your first priority.

A business plan also helps in ensuring the long-term success of your business. It shows measurable actions and results that allow you to do the tracking and strategy adjustments that lead to success. Without a plan, you may not achieve your goals and, worse yet, you may end up out of business. A business plan needs to be viewed as a document that you review regularly and update as needed to accommodate lessons learned and changes in circumstances. Think about your business plan as being your proposal—the document that you are going to show investors/loan officers in order to raise capital.

First, keep in mind that whenever you ask somebody for money, whether it's for a small personal loan or a large amount of money to finance your business, you are involved in a selling situation. You have to prepare a sales presentation, just as if you were getting ready to sell a car. Within the sales presentation, you must have all the facts and figures. You must anticipate the questions and the possible objections of the prospective lender, with answers or explanations. Finally, you must package it as impressively as you would prepare yourself for a presentation to the largest bank in your area.

The more money you ask for, the more knowledgeable the people you want to borrow from will be, and the more detailed and organized your proposal must be. This shouldn't cause you too much worry, however, because you can hire an accountant to help you put the numbers and details together properly. Look at this way, the more money you request for your business, the more your lenders or prospective investors are going to want to know about you, your planning, and your business. They want to be impressed with the fact that you've done your homework. They want to see that you've researched everything and documented your facts and figures. They want to be assured by your presentation that investing in your business will make money for them. It's just that simple at the bottom line. Unless you can instill confidence in them with your business plan and loan or investment proposal, they are just not going to give much thought to your request for money.

Your business plan should detail as much as possible the product or products you plan to sell. How you are going to produce or manufacture the product, your costs, inventory cost, if you are purchasing them from a supplier, who is going to sell those products for you, how they are going to be sold, the attendant cost, when you expect to recoup your initial investment, your plans for growth or expansion, and the total amount you are going to need to make it all work according to your plan. Your business plan must be detailed, complete with projected income and expense figures for at least the first year of business. You'll also need a balance sheet describing your net worth—the value of what you own compared to the amount of money you owe.

You'll also have to prove your stability and money management talent relative to how successful you've been in paying off past obligations. If you've had credit problems in the past, get them cleaned up or at least explained on your file at your local credit bureau office. Under the law, credit bureaus are required to give you all the information they have about you in your files, and it's your right to correct any errors or enter explanations regarding negative reports on your credit. Do this without fail because prospective lenders or investors will definitely check your credit history.

So, now you have your balance sheet prepared. Your credit is reorganized in a light that is favorable to you. Your business plan with cost and income projected during the coming three years has been developed. Now you are ready to start looking for lenders or investors. Your first stop isn't the local bank. Instead, you should look to your family and friends for financial help. The best place to get capital into your organization is with those who are closest to you. Usually, they are the easiest ones to work with because their terms are a little more realistic. They are not trying to take every dollar back out of your business. And they typically don't try to restrict your ability to operate your company. That can happen with many venture capitalist firms, which can often restrict the way you operate and tie you up in a way you don't want to be. So it's often best to start off getting financing from those who are closest to you.

But just because these people may know you, it doesn't mean that you can be anything less than businesslike with them. Approach them in a businesslike manner. Tell them about your idea or plans, and ask them for a loan. Agree to sign a formal statement to pay them back in three, five, or ten years with interest. When you have your proposal assembled, you might even want to think about a limited partnership or even a general partnership arrangement as a way to finance your project. In any kind of partnership, each partner shares in the profit of the company. But in a limited kind of partnership, each person's loss liability is limited to the amount of money he or she initially invested.

Another common method of obtaining business financing is through second mortgage loans on home or existing piece of property. Say you purchased a home ten years ago for thirty-five thousand dollars and today the assessed valuation as eighty-five thousand dollars with an outstanding mortgage of twenty-five thousand dollars. A lender may consider your home to be security or collateral for a loan for up to sixty thousand dollars. In many cases, this is the easiest and surest way of getting the money needed for a business investment. And it makes sense—you've got a net worth available in your house that is doing nothing but sitting there.

While there is a risk involved with this approach the most important point to note is that all business opportunities involve risk and sacrifice. It's up to you to determine the feasibility of your success with your proposed venture, and then decide on the best possible way to proceed.

In every instance where you run into reluctance from the part of potential lenders, try exploring the feasibilities of two-name or co-signed loans. You can have a business partner, a supplier, or a friend sign with you. You can usually borrow against any collateral such as stocks, bonds, *time* certificates, business equipment, or other Real Estate, and in this way give greater confidence to the lender in your ability to repay the loan.

Whenever you can show a contract from someone who has agreed to purchase a certain amount of your products or services during a specified period of time, you have another important piece of paper that most lenders will accept as collateral.

Another possibility might be to get a bank or a firm that has loaned you money in the past to guarantee your loan. In this case, they simply guarantee that they will lend you the money in the future, if ever the need should arise. Remember that going straight to your neighborhood bank, applying for a business loan, and walking out with the money is just about the most unlikely of all your possibilities. Banks want to lend money, and they must lend money in order to stay in business. But most banks are notoriously conservative and extremely reluctant to lend you money unless you have a regular income that guarantees repayment. If and when you approach a bank for a business loan, you will need all your papers in order—your financial statements, business plan, credit history, and all the endorsements you can get that point to your success with your planned enterprise. In addition, it would be a good idea to take along your accountant, just to ensure the banker that your plan is verifiable. In the end, you will find that it all boils down to whether or not the bank officer studying your application is sold on you as a good credit risk. It is paramount, therefore, that you impress the banker, not only with your proposal, but with your appearance and personality as well. In dealing with bankers, never show an attitude or doubt or apology. Always be positive and sure of yourself.

Your best bet in attempting to get a business loan from a bank is to deal with commercial banks. These are the banks that specialize in investment loans for businesses, Real Estate, and even venture programs. Look in your local yellow pages. Call and ask for an appointment with the manager, and then explore with him or her the possibilities of a loan for your project. One of the nice things about commercial banks is that even though they may not be able to approve a loan for your business idea, they will almost always give you a list of names of businesspeople who might be interested in looking over your proposal for investment purposes.

Many commercial banks stage investment lectures and seminars for the general public. If you find one that does, be sure to attend. You'll meet a lot of local businesspeople; some may be able to help you with your business plan, including finding money to invest. Many entrepreneurs are so anxious to get funding that they jump at the first opportunity presented to them. It is important that you get the money at terms suitable to you.

Don't overlook the possibility of advertising for a lender or investor in your local papers. Also, consider placing your ads in national publications. You will reach people looking for investments. Other avenues to seriously consider are: foundations that offer grants, local dental and medical investment groups, legal investment groups, business associations, trust companies, Friends, relatives, individuals, savings and loan associations, insurance companies, finance companies, mortgage companies, small business investment companies, venture capital firms, state government financing sources, pension funds, private foundations, and government agencies, starting with the SBA.

Check your phone book to find an U.S. Small Business Administration (SBA) office near you. The SBA is the federal agency created specifically to assist and counsel owners of small businesses. The SBA is set up to help owners of commercial enterprises develop their businesses. In dealing with the SBA, you actually deal with a standard commercial bank, just as you would if you went to the bank. The SBA can actually guarantee your loan for the bank. The bank may deny your request for a loan saying that your business doesn't have a history or you personally have a poor credit rating. But the bank will then go to the SBA and get it to approve the loan. If you default on that loan, the bank is in the clear because it can go to the federal government to get that loan paid for. The result is that banks become very liberal in helping small businesses get started by offering a lower interest rate or by giving you credit they otherwise would not give.

While you should check the various programs available from the SBA website, your first step is with the bank. Work through the process of getting a loan with the bank, letting the loan officer know you are going to go through the SBA. What the loan officer will do is submit your loan proposal to the SBA. Once the SBA approves it, the bank will approve your loan.

Speaking of government money, every state has Small Business Development Centers that can recommend the right government grant program for you. All

Development Centers offer free counseling to anyone wishing to start or expand a business. These services include seminars, workshops, business planning, feasibility studies, marketing research, management analyses, sales techniques, financing exporting, inventory control, accounting, record keeping, and grant applications. Refer to your telephone directory under state offices and contact your Small Business Development Center: http://www.sba.gov/content/small-business-development-centers-sbdcs-0.

Also look at small business investment companies. These organizations can provide you with the capital you need by giving you a free loan, making a stock investment in your business, or offering a combination of the two. Small business investment companies are in the business of making money, just as any other business.

The biggest difference between them and other investors is that they are privately managed firms that are licensed and partially financed by the Small Business Administration. All of their transactions are regulated by the government. Their success depends on the growth and profit of companies in which they own stock. They often give money in exchange for stock in a company. Their loans usually carry lower interest rates than commercial banks. Straight loan repayments are carried over a longer period of time than with other lenders. Most businesses are eligible, especially those that are 50 percent minority owned. For a complete listing of the thousands of small business investment companies, visit your local public library, check the SBA's website, or ask your banker, lawyer, or accountant.

The bottom line is this: you must have a well-researched and detailed business plan. You must have all your documents and projections put together in an impressive presentation and you will have to be the one who does all the final selling of your proposal to the investor or lender. Place a lot of emphasis on your appearance, personality, and attitude because, make no mistake about it, they *all* count.

Once your corporation is established, the need for cash to fund ongoing cash flow will arise. Let's suppose you just started your business and went to your bank to get a loan through your corporation based on your credit history because you want to avoid any future liability. If your corporation was just formed, it has no credit history, no tax returns, no financial statements, and you will not get a loan for it. The bank may lend the corporation money if you give a personal guarantee. That means the bank will lend your business money based on your having excellent personal credit and giving a guarantee personally. If the corporation declares bankruptcy, then you are personally responsible for the loan.

How does that sound? Probably not very good. Is there a way to get around personal guarantees? You bet. You can build up the credit worthiness of your corporation. What if your own personal credit is less than satisfactory? In that case, the goal would be to establish corporate credit and obtain a loan through the merits of your business's credit without personal guarantee.

Any time a corporation applies for a loan or fills out an application, a certain amount of corporate privacy will be lost. This means that if the corporation has access to money, and privacy is important to the corporation, then there is probably no reason to go through the process to establish corporate credit. What if you are in a position where you need corporate privacy and a credit rating to borrow money? Then what will you do? The answer is to have more than one business. One business or corporation goes through the credit process so that when it needs to borrow twenty-five thousand dollars, for example, it can do so. That corporation will lose some of its privacy in this process. You can create a separate corporation, or even several others, and can be involved in that business transaction yet keep your business affairs as private as possible. These other corporations can even borrow money from the main corporation that has gone through the process of establishing an excellent credit rating. This will accomplish the best of both worlds—obtaining credit yet maintaining personal privacy.

You may already be familiar with the personal credit bureaus, TRW, Equifax, and Trans Union. These are the agencies from which you'd obtain a personal credit file on yourself. You may be very surprised at the mistakes in these files. You should receive a report of your information and clean up any mistakes in your personal credit history. Through incorporation, you can separate yourself from your business and protect your personal assets from any business liabilities.

While it is possible to build a business credit profile for a sole proprietorship or partnership, you and your family are still personally responsible for all the debt your business may incur. Instead, look at building your business credit as a corporation or a limited liability company (LLC). When you incorporate, you benefit from: protection of your personal assets, the ability to raise capital and build credit faster, lower tax liabilities, limited liabilities of owners and officers, 100 percent tax deductible insurance, 100 percent medical expense reimbursement, stock ownership that makes it easier to transfer assets, greater credibility through a corporate image, and lowered audit risk.

A corporation must earn its credit worthiness just as an individual must. Thus, the first step is to understand who is doing your business rating. There are two business credit reporting agencies in the United States that lenders and financial institutions rely on for information to grant credit—Dunn and Bradstreet (D&B) and Experian. However, for companies, Dunn and Bradstreet is the main organization that maintains credit files on corporations. If you apply to a bank for a loan for your business, you can almost guarantee that the bank will call D&B for a credit report on your company. The first step in acquiring corporate credit is to call D&B and obtain a number from them. Their phone number is 800-333-0505. You will be asked the following questions: your business's name, telephone number, mailing and physical address, type of business, sales and net worth, number of employees, condition of the company's starting capital, company's background, corporate location (headquarters), items for sale or services offered, names of corporate officers, how long your corporation has been in business, whether or not it is minority owned, name of the contact person and his or her corporate title, and five venders as references.

Lenders will use D&B information in different ways. Most will manage with a lower score from D&B if you are requiring smaller amount of money, say, fifty thousand dollars or less. The key is to understand that every corporate lender is different. Most will have more flexibility when economic times are good, and are therefore more eager to lend money. Shop your needs around to various lending institutions to get the best deal for you and your corporation.

Another step you must take is to obtain an employer identification number (EIN). This is the number the IRS requires when filing tax returns for a corporation and for employee purposes. Most banks will not allow you to open a bank account for your business unless you have this number. An EIN must be obtained for an LLC as well as a corporation. Even if you already have an EIN as a sole proprietor, this number is not usable for the new corporation or LLC. You must obtain a new one.

Once you have the EIN, look at establishing a corporate credit card. American Express should be one of your first stops for this. You can obtain an American Express card or an Optima card, which works like a regular Visa or MasterCard. There is no fee for the Optima corporate card, although it doesn't have some of the corporate benefits that the regular corporate credit cards offer. Here is some of the information they will ask for: the physical address and phone number of the corporation, and the name of the individual responsible personally for the account. Yes, you'll have to give your Social Security number. Basically, this is a personal guarantee to American Express. Credit references will be required. This means the corporate bank account or any corporate trade references. If the corporation is brand new and has none of these, you will have to give personal credit references. If that's not good, then you'll have to wait a few months until you establish some corporate references. The credit limit will be based on the credit history of the company or individual. Usually, you will have at least a one-thousand-dollar credit limit on American Express. Each month that you pay off your balance on time, you will get up to a 10 percent increase in the amount of credit.

Another opportunity for your company to build credit comes with secured credit cards. If you can't get a normal credit card for your business, you may be able to get a debit card with your bank or maybe a secured credit card. You put in a few hundred dollars and in return you get a line of credit. It's secure to a certain extent and you can use it to conduct business. Remember, just as in your personal life, it's very difficult to exist in business today without having these forms of credit available to you, whether you need to rent a car, buy an airline ticket, or travel in any other way.

Leasing companies will help you build credit. If, for example, you need a computer, a photocopier, or other expensive machinery, you can set up a lease with the supplier. Most of these suppliers have special programs specially designed for new businesses. Establishing a lease creates a credit history for your organization. Gateway and Dell offer these programs for businesses, while stores like Office Depot offer leases for office furniture. Cell phones and even cars can be arranged for using these types of deals. This frees up cash for your everyday operations and at the same time builds up credit for your company.

Let's explore giving a personal guarantee for your corporation. Earlier, I spoke about obtaining corporate credit by giving personal guarantees. Can you get around this? The answer is yes, depending on where you are getting your loan, as well as your skills as a negotiator.

One option for you is to offer alternative collateral instead of a personal guarantee. Convince your supplier or vender to accept a security interest on assets of the business instead, or maybe they can accept a guarantee from an affiliated corporation. Remember, find a creditor who wants your business. If you show them some cash up front, they may be more than willing to forgo the personal guarantee; if they won't, their competitor might. Maybe you can get only half the credit line without a personal guarantee. Instead of ten thousand dollars, maybe you can get only five thousand to start. Ask the creditor if the personal guarantee could be dropped if you could have, say, a "probation" period of six months. The name of the game is to negotiate. Remember, avoid giving creditors a personal guarantee, no matter how much they insist on one. If you absolutely *have* to sign a personal guarantee, make sure your partner(s) signs also. The goal is to avoid personal guarantees as much as possible, and to quickly pay off any loans that have a personal guarantee, in order to preserve your own credit rating.

So far, I've been talking about raising money, and getting corporate credit as a loan, which needs to be paid back at some point, even if it is far in the future. The other option is getting equity from investors who will put up money in exchange for a piece or share of your business. If you expect to seek money from investors, even if they are family members, friends, or business associates, there is a substantial advantage in forming a corporation. Unlike a lender who in return for providing money receives a promise that you will repay it with interest, an investor becomes a part-owner of the business. While it's possible to form a partnership and make an investor a partner or to form a limited liability company and make an investor a member, its often more practical to form a corporation and make the investor a shareholder. That little piece of paper that the corporation issues—the stock certificate—is tangible proof of the shareholder's ownership interest, and is something that most investors have come to expect. Put another way, if you offer an investor a partnership interest or an LLC interest, you are more likely to run into resistance than if you offer him stock in the corporation. Keep in mind that shareholders don't necessarily have to have equal rights to elect the board of directors or to receive dividends.

To distinguish between various types of shareholders, you can issue different classes of stocks with different rights. For example, offer common voting shares to the initial owners who will be working in the business, non-voting shares for key employees to retain their loyalty to the business, non-voting preferred shares to outside investors, giving them a preference if dividends are declared or the corporation is sold.

To repeat this key point: the fact that the corporate structure makes it relatively easy to distinguish between different investors by issuing different classes of stock is a real advantage. Issuing stock can be a way to motivate employees. Employees who get stock are often willing to work for a lower salary, making investment capital go further in the early days of the business's life.

Another advantage of setting up a corporation is that it gives you credibility. It shows investors that you have a legal structure in place. They will understand that there are stockholders in your company, there are officers, there are directors, and there are people who manage your company, even if you are the only one who runs all those positions. All of these give you the necessary credibility with any type of investor. As an entrepreneur, you must keep in mind your credit needs as your business develops and evolves.

One of the biggest problems with fast-growing companies is cash flow. You might have a wonderful business and be selling a lot of your product, but you might have very little immediate cash coming in. Maybe you are generous and are allowing payment in sixty or ninety days, or maybe customers are slow in repaying you. In the meantime, you still have to pay your employees and you still have to pay the rent and other bills. Therefore, you want to start as early as possible establishing the good credit history you might need to draw into the future.

Start putting your plans for your business on paper right now. Think about what amount of money you will need for financing, and start keeping your eyes open as you go about your daily business for creative sources for financing, even when your business is up and running. Keep thinking about building the type of business credit you will need throughout the life of your corporation. Doing different things at the same time, running a business, looking after your corporation, and slowly building up the value of that company takes time and lots of knowledge, which is where my business can step in to help you along your path to success.

"There is a trade-off for the entrepreneurial life and its opportunities and rewards that the entrepreneur and his family must pay - and often the payment is demanded at difficult times or under difficult circumstances.

The entrepreneur does not have one boss to call in sick to; he has dozens or hundreds of bosses to whom he has made express or implicit promises and owes performance, who rightly do not and cannot care about the entrepreneur's personal life or family obligations.

The only way to have the "freedoms" that come with an "ordinary" life of salaried employment or hourly wages is to choose that life and accept its financial and other limitations and disadvantages.

Those around you may understand, but they may never fully accept it."

Life Is Rich
www.AskNateScott.com
904.838.2623

CHAPTER 8
Guarding Your Financial Privacy

Luke 10:23-24 "*23 And he turned him unto his disciples, and said privately, Blessed are the eyes which see the things that ye see: 24 For I tell you, that many prophets and kings have desired to see those things which ye see, and have not seen them; and to hear those things which ye hear, and have not heard them.*"

In this chapter, I will write about something that is very important but that many people don't even give a passing thought to—guarding your financial privacy to ensure your financial success.

Your financial privacy isn't just about protecting yourself, but also protecting your hard-earned assets. This program stresses that it's not just how much money you make, but also how much you get to keep. Whether it's credit card protection and identity theft or protecting yourself and your business from lawsuits, there are lots of risks out there that you have to protect yourself from.

Privacy strategies can help lower your profile. These strategies can protect you from financial crimes and achieve a level of comfort from knowing your privacy isn't easily violated and at the fingertip of someone else's computer.

Where is the best place to start? How about the one place that is often used to tie together your credit history, employment history, taxation records, and literally thousands of other documents? I am talking about your Social Security number. Today, it seems that just about everybody wants your Social Security number. They use it to see if you pay your bills and to keep track of you through name and address changes and to access your credit rating. But companies also use your Social Security number to develop marketing lists that they can sell to other companies. A list with numbers is more valuable than one without. Why should you care who sees your Social Security number? The more people who see it, the more susceptible you are to identity theft. Unscrupulous people can fraudulently use your name and credit report to steal money.

Identity theft costs American companies billions of dollars every year. These costs are eventually passed on to consumers, including you. So who has the right to ask for your Social Security number? While any business can ask for your Social Security number, there are very few that can actually demand it; examples include: the motor vehicle department, and the U.S. welfare system. Also, Social Security numbers are required for transactions involving taxes, so that means banks, brokerages, employers and the like also have a legitimate need for your Social Security number (SSN). Most other businesses have no legal right to demand your number. While there is no law stopping a business from asking for your number, neither is there a law requiring you to provide it.

If you are asked for your SSN, ask if an alternative piece of identification can be acceptable. If it isn't, you can just refuse to do business there. Bear in mind that there is a possibility businesses will refuse to provide whatever product or service you are seeking, but chances are good that many companies that routinely ask for Social Security numbers, will do business with you even if they can't have yours.

One of the biggest problems associated with misuse of Social Security numbers is identity theft. Most people think that identity theft can't or won't happen to them. Identity theft is one of those things you are probably not very concerned about if it hasn't happened to you already, but it's a frequently occurring crime. In 2001, there were approximately five hundred thousand identity theft victims who actually filled a police report.

It costs banks and credit card companies about five billion dollars because they ultimately picked up the tab, but you as a consumer don't get away scot-free either. The average victim will spend 1,374 dollars and 175 hours cleaning up their credit report. That's a great deal of time and money out of a person's own pocket.

It's surprisingly simple to assume someone's identity today. If you go to the grocery store and write a check for seventy dollars, the check has your full name and address and maybe even your phone number. It also has the full name and address of the bank where the check is drawn, as well as your account number. Maybe the clerk asks for your driver's license, which may be the same as your Social Security number in your state. So they write your Social Security number on the face of the check and they ask for date of birth and a work phone number. They can now call and find out where you are employed. Don't forget that hundreds of pairs of eyes can see this check—people at the grocery store and at the check clearinghouse. Then it goes back to the payee bank, and if you don't get your checks in your statements, it goes to a company that shreds them. So much information exists on just that little piece of paper. And this is just *one* way identity theft can take place.

Years ago, identity theft was less involved. A crook would think that if they can get enough information, they can apply for a Visa, use it for a couple of weeks, and then throw it away. But today the crook thinks, "If I can get enough information, I can get a cell phone, a car, and then a mortgage. I can go to work for a company under contract labor and have somebody else pay the taxes. According to a new study of more than one thousand identity theft arrests in the United States by a Michigan

State professor, as many as 70 percent of all cases begin with the theft of personal data from a company by an employee. Think about this the next time you are structuring your financial affairs.

There is some help from the government on this. In 2004, President Bush signed the Identity Theft Penalty Enhancement Act, which increases the federal penalty for identity theft from three to five years. It also adds five years to prison sentences for those convicted of using another person's identity to commit an act of terrorism. In addition, the Act made aggravated identity theft a crime. People convicted of using someone else's identity and committing a felony will have an additional two years tacked on to their sentence(s).

We live in a time that, if you make it easy to steal from you, chances are someone will. Using the information I am sharing with you today, you can be much smarter about your financial affairs. These nine steps will help reduce your risk of identity theft.

1. *Guard your Social Security number.* Your SSN is the key to your credit report and banking accounts, and is the prime target of criminals. Do not print your Social Security number on your checks. After applying for a loan, credit card, rental, or anything else that requires a credit report, request that your Social Security number on the application be truncated or completely obliterated and your original credit report be shredded before your eyes or returned to you once a decision has been made.

2. *Monitor your credit report.* Credit reports can alert you to activity in your financial records. Check your records often.

3. *Buy a shredder and use it.* Identity thieves may use your garbage to obtain personal information. Shred all old bank and credit statements as well as junk mail such as credit card offers before trashing them.

4. *Remove your name from marketing lists.* The three credit reporting bureaus, Equifax, Experian, and Trans Union all maintain marketing lists that may contain your information. Contact the agencies to remove your name from these lists. You should also add your name to the name deletion list of the direct marketing association mail preference service and telephone preference service used by banks and other marketers. Removing your name from these lists reduces the number of pre-approved credit offers you receive.

5. *Watch what you carry in your wallet.* Do not keep your Social Security card in your wallet or extra credit cards or other important identity documents except when needed. These documents can give thieves ready access to your accounts.

6. *Keep duplicate records.* Place the contents of your wallet on a photocopy machine. Copy both sides of your license and credit cards so you have all the account numbers, expiration dates, and phone numbers in case your wallet\or purse is stolen.
7. *Mail payments from safe locations.* Do not mail bill payments and checks from home. They can be stolen from your mailbox and washed clean in chemicals. Take them to the post office.
8. *Monitor your Social Security activity.* Order your Social Security earnings and benefits statements once a year to check for fraud.
9. *Know whom you are talking to.* Never give your credit card numbers or personal information to anyone on the phone, unless you have initiated the call and trust that business.

Before we leave this subject, here are some recent changes to the law that will help protect you from identity fraud:

You now have a right to free credit reports. Instead of paying eight to ten dollars for each, you will be able to order a free copy of your history from each of the three credit bureaus every year. Identity theft victims can order two copies from each bureau during the year in which the theft occurred.

Lenders and credit bureaus are now forbidden from reporting negative information that results from identity theft. This one seems to be pretty straightforward, but identity theft victims about the bureau's practice of reinserting negative information after the victims have spent months getting their credit reports cleared. Lenders must honor fraud alerts by verifying an applicant's identity. Consumers who have been victims of identity theft or who worry that they might have long been able to put fraud alerts on their credit reports. These alerts are supposed to tip lenders off that the consumer wants to be contacted by phone before credit is granted. Good idea, right? But some lenders routinely ignore fraud alerts. They'd rather extend credit even to thieves than slow down their credit granting machines. Lenders now have to contact consumers before granting credit when a fraud alert is on the file, either by phone or other reasonable steps.

All of this helps, but remember, the first step is yours. That's why it's so important to check your credit reports regularly. It's often the only way you'll know that bogus accounts have been opened in your name.

What else can you do to keep your identity safe? Destroy private records and statements. Tear, or if you prefer, shred credit card statements, solicitation, and other documents that contain private financial information. Empty your mailbox quickly so criminals don't have a chance to snatch credit card pitches. Consider locking your mailbox. Don't carry your Social Security card with you or any card that may have your number. Don't put your number on your checks. Leave your driver's license number off your checks as well. Never leave ATM or gas station receipts behind. Worried about credit card scamming? Pay with cash as often as possible.

When making an online purchase, look in the lower right hand corner of your browser window. If you see the icon of a lock, that means you are dealing with a secure site. If you don't see one, you'd be safer finding another merchant. Also, check out website privacy policies. Shy away from sites that don't specifically say that they won't pass your name and information around to others. Stick to well-known retailers or sites that others have used to their satisfaction. Use only one credit card for online purchases. That way, if something amiss happens, it will be easier to spot on your bill. Be more defensive with personal information. Ask salespeople and others if information such as Social Security numbers or driver's licenses is absolutely necessary.

Ask anyone who does require your Social Security number, for instance your insurance company, what their privacy policy is, and whether you can arrange for the organization not to share that information with anyone else.

And how about the phone and the computer? The direct marketing association maintains a service through which consumers can remove themselves from phone, mail, and e-mail solicitation lists used by association members. Here are the steps:

To be removed from the mailing list, write to Mail Preference Service, Direct Marketing Association, P.O. Box 9008, Farmingdale, New York 11735. When giving your name, use full names, nick names, and any other combination that a solicitor may use.

To be removed from the phone list, send your name, address, and phone number to Telephone Preference Service, DMA, Box 9014 Farmingdale, New York 11735. Make sure you provide all phone numbers you might use. If you get an unwanted e-mail, don't use the remove me option that many such e-mails offer. In a lot of cases, all that means is that the e-mail has hit an active address and that only means more solicitation. Set up an e-mail garbage address. Use one e-mail address for transactions and other activities that may lead to spam. Use another for all private communication.

Getting a lot of telephone solicitation? Just tell them not to call again. The telephone consumer protection Act of 1991 stipulates that they have to do so if you ask. If they happen to call again, you may be able to sue them for five hundred dollars in a private Writ of Action in your local court.

Contact your credit card company and find out how to take part in their opt-out program. This prevents your name from being passed around to solicitors and other companies with whom your cardholder deals.

All of these things will help keep your business, money, and financial affairs private, just as they should be. One of the main reasons we look at financial privacy is because of the litigation explosion that's taking place throughout the world. The United States is the only nation that actually takes cases on contingency or on commission. This means that if you go to a lawyer's office and say that you have been damaged or injured, they can take your case on a percentage basis. If you win one million dollars, they might take up to 50 percent of your settlement, depending on how far they go with it.

Another interesting statistic is that more than 94 percent of all lawsuits in the entire world are filed in the United States and many of those are on the West Coast. So, if you are living on the West Coast, you are living in the most litigious section of the country.

One of the best ways to take care of yourself and protect yourself is to lower your profile and achieve some privacy in case litigation is filed against you. Many people start thinking about this once they've gone through the stress, misery, and the financial agony of dealing with lawsuits but the time to think about ways of protecting yourself from litigation is right now—before you are involved in a lawsuit. I am sure you have read about or heard about the more famous cases such as the woman who sued McDonalds because her coffee was too hot. What did the first jury award her? They awarded her $2.2 million! There is another case in Florida where armed robbers went into a convenience store and stole money out of a till and ran out. They jumped into the vehicle waiting for them and sped off. At the same time, the attendant who was behind the counter ran out after them to get their license plate number and chase them down. As they sped away, they crashed into a median. They damaged their car and a couple of people inside the car got hurt. Well, guess what happened? They ended up suing the owner of the convenience store, because that store's attendant had run after the robbers, put them in a position where they had to go fast, and they crashed. Now, this seems ridiculous and absurd, but it was a successful suit. The convenience store had to pay the money.

How about the burglar who broke into a home through the skylight, fell, and broke his neck. Who did he sue? You've got it—the homeowner. Are these things ridiculous? Yes. Did they take place? Absolutely, these kinds of things happen all the time.

Now, as business owners and professionals, you have to be concerned about these cases. There are numerous cases that many of us would consider frivolous lawsuits. But people actually make careers out of suing other people. You could spend ten thousand dollars easily. In fact, that oftentimes is just a minor retainer for an attorney to represent you, if you are being sued in business or professional life or if you are a doctor or a dentist. Law firms will ask for an initial retainer of ten thousand dollars. However, you will often find that just paying five thousand or ten thousand dollars will get rid of these frivolous cases.

Let's go back to the information I covered at the beginning of this chapter. Let's say that a group of people are thinking about suing you. The first thing they are going to want to know is what you have. For instance, they will want to know if you own Real Estate. They will run a profile on you and do an asset search. Sometimes, this is done by an attorney. If you find that you've got credit card bills of ten thousand, twenty-five thousand dollars, and they find out that you are living in a two-hundred-thousand-dollar house, and you've got a mortgage for a hundred and eighty thousand, there is really no reason to initiate civil litigation against you because there is nothing to take. So, they are going to search for your assets.

And how do they find those assets? Well, there are national search companies that can be hired very inexpensively, and most lawyers know how to tap into these organizations. They advertise in law journals and they can search just about any database—city databases for business licenses, country databases for Real Estate that you might own, state databases for business entities that you might have, or any kind of fillings for leans against you. They can get into tax databases better, and they can do this in all fifty states in a very short period of time due to how fast information can be processed with computers today. They can find out what your mortgage balance is on your home right now, what your credit card balance is, and they can identify how much you have.

If you have a cabin in another state or a piece of Real Estate, maybe just some land that you like to visit, the best way to hold this is not to hold it in your own name. You can use trusts or limited partnerships or even a corporation to hold your assets. What you are doing is legally lowering your profile and, hopefully, lowering the likelihood that litigants are going to track you down.

You wouldn't walk around with your financial statements taped to your forehead, would you? So why would you have your most valuable assets exposed to public scrutiny? Anyone can go down to a county court house or recorder's office and look up the owners of any property. Real Estate records are now computerized, so all of your Real Estate holdings can be located at the touch of a button.

Any mortgages on your property will be recorded as well. Most recorded mortgages will state the amount of the original principal balance and the date the mortgage payments began. All one has to do is figure out the balance of your mortgage and subtract that amount from the market value of your house. Now they know how much equity you have and hence whether suing you is worthwhile.

If tenants or creditors are contemplating suing you, they will make an appointment with a lawyer. Unless they can afford an attorney by the hour, they will likely seek a contingency fee lawyer. Contingency fee lawyers do not charge by the hour, they charge a percentage of whatever they collect. Most contingency fee lawyers will not take a case unless there is something from which to collect. If you have no Real Estate in your name, then finding out your ownership interest will not be easy for a typical lawyer. It's not that lawyers are lazy; it's simply a matter of allocation of resources. Lawyers focus on cases they can win and collect from. If they don't find any assets in your name and there is no other apparent de-pocket, they probably won't take the case. As you can see, appearing broke is one of the best lawsuit repellants that money can buy.

There is another problem with owning Real Estate in your own name. If a judgment is obtained against you and filed in any county in which you own Real Estate, all Real Estate in that county will have a lien attached to it. You cannot sell or refinance any property in that county since no title insurance company will guarantee a clean title. You are stuck until you pay off the lien.

A land trust can be an excellent investment vehicle for you. A land trust is a revocable living trust used to title ownership of Real Estate. The title to the property is held in the name of a trustee who is forbidden to reveal the beneficial owner. The beneficial owner—beneficiary—can be an individual corporation or other entity for further protection. A land trust, if properly set up and implemented, will hide your name from the public records. No one will know who owns the property but you, your attorney, and the trustee. If a judgment is entered against you, a lean will not automatically attach to the property, since the title is not in your name.

There are other ways to lower your profile. If you own Real Estate, when you visit your tenants don't drive your Mercedes—if you have one. Drive some old crank of a car. Tenants will think that even if they have a problem with you there is nothing to take from you. Make sure you are not wearing flashy jewelry such as an expensive watch—anything fancy. In fact, most wealthy people in this country who understand how bad litigation is and how to protect themselves don't have a high profile existence. They are not driving the fanciest cars and they are not out there flashing money around. Lowering your profile is something you must think about.

So what can you do about it? Let's look closely at the solutions to all of these.

You want to separate your assets from you. You want to get them out of your name as best as you can. And that can be done through varied business entities or legal entities themselves. Sometimes, it's just using a corporate structure to run a business from, or maybe you have a piece of Real Estate that's earning income for you. Use a business structure in every situation that you can, and use some privacy in creating that business structure. Let's say you have a cabin. It's your second residence somewhere. You can put that into a trust or put it into a limited partnership. The key to wealth-building is all about control, not ownership, and that's the most important thing. If you control assets and can direct assets, that's one thing, and nobody can take that away from you. However, if you own those assets, they are yours, but if someone can win a judgment against you, he or she can go after any assets you own. The real objective with privacy and holding assets and managing businesses, is to control those assets but not to own those assets. Get rid of your ego that wants to brag about your wealth and display it all the time, because it's that ego that will get you into trouble.

Let's look at some of the most common pitfalls that lead to liability in lawsuits for small business owners and how to avoid them.

Pitfall #1: *Doing business as a sole proprietor.* Most people who go into business do so as a sole proprietor. This means that they are doing business as an individual—DBA, dba, d.b.a., or d/b/a, which stands for Doing Business As.

This scenario offers absolutely no asset protection, not to mention poor tax benefits. If the business is sued, all the personal assets of the individual are at risk. For only a few hundred dollars, you can form a corporation to do your business or to trade. If properly maintained, the corporation will shield your personal assets if the business is sued or goes bankrupt.

Pitfall #2: *Doing business as a general partnership.* Doing business with a partner can be even worse than doing business as a sole proprietor. A partnership is formed when two or more people decide to do business together for profit. It does not require a formal partnership agreement or the filling of any official documents, although it often done that way. A partnership can be created, even if the parties did not intend one to exist.

Here is the problem with a general partnership. If your partner does something foolish, you become liable. That's right—if you allow your partner to commit the partnership to a contract, the partnership and its partners can be held liable for that debt. If your partner is negligent or incurs a debt on behalf of the partnership, you are on the hook, even if your partner files for bankruptcy. If you intend on doing business with a partner, consider a corporation or other limited liability entity. It's just as easy to set up for two people as it is for one.

Pitfall #3: *Using a corporation improperly.* A corporation is good, but only if used properly. Many people pay a lawyer up to one thousand dollars to set up a corporation, then they take the corporation's minute book and stick it in the closet. The corporation will not shield you from personal liability if you do not follow corporate formalities (noted in the previous module in this series). Even worse, if the IRS audits you, it can set aside the corporation and call it a sham, and hold you personally liable for the taxes. At least once a year, have your attorney and/or your tax advisor review your corporate records and practices.

Pitfall #4: *Personal guarantees.* In some situations, such as a bank loan or a line of credit, it's inevitable that you must sign personally. However, it is not necessary to give a personal guarantee in every situation simply because they have requested it. Often vendors of your business will request that you sign a personal guarantee of corporate liability. If they are not extending you credit, you should simply refuse.

For example, if a landlord requests a personal guarantee on a lease, offer a larger security deposit instead, or you can negotiate for it after two years of prompt payment, your personal guarantee is not necessary.

If you chose to sign personally on an obligation, do not make the mistake of allowing your spouse to co-sign with you. Unless your spouse is involved in your business, there is no reason for a vender or a bank to require your spouse's personal guarantee.

Pitfall #5: *Failure to maintain adequate insurance.* Do not be cheap when it comes to insurance. Insurance will help protect you in most circumstances. If you keep the minimum insurance, increase the liability limits. You can usually double your liability insurance for a relatively small amount. Keep in mind that if your insurance is not adequate to cover a claim, the injured party can go after your personal or unincorporated business assets for the difference. Insurance also gives you an attorney in the event that you are sued, even if the claim is settled before trial. The duty of an insurer to defend you and pay for your lawyer is much broader than its duty to indemnify and pay for claims against you. Even if the lawsuit is completely bogus, the insurance company will provide you with a lawyer, saving you thousands of dollars.

Pitfall #6: *Sexual harassment and discrimination in your business.* Sexual harassment and discrimination of any type is an important issue. If you own a company with an employee, be aware of what goes on. Even if you don't engage personally in any contact that is harassing in nature, you can be sued if your company permits the hostile environment. Make certain you have written company policies that are given to all your employees that specifically states that sexual harassment will not be tolerated. Set up an internal complaint and investigation procedure within your company. Immediately investigate and resolve any issues within your company, especially those that involve people of the opposite sex. Be especially aware of these events if you have a company picnic or office party.

Pitfall #7: *Using independent contractors.* If you regularly pay contract employees, you may be trending on thin ice. If your independent contractor commits a negligent act and a third party is injured, you can be held liable. The problem with this area of law is that it does not matter whether you thought the individual was an independent contractor or an employee. The law presumes an individual is an employee by balancing some of the following factors. Do your contract employees work your hours or theirs? Did they use your tools or do they have their own? Do they work for other people or just for you? Did you personally supervise the work? Did you pay them daily, weekly, or upon completion? Was there a written contract? These are only some of the factors, but you can get a general idea of what factors are relevant. If the court considers the individuals to be your employees, you are responsible for their actions.

Pitfall #8: *Failure to get it in writing.* Always leave a paper trail. Whenever you speak with representatives of companies—the IRS or any government organization—get it in writing. If they won't give it to you in writing, send them a follow-up letter summarizing your conversation. Their failure to object with content may be deemed as an admission of what the letter states. Keep a copy in your file in case you have to prove the oral conversation in court. Remember, it's not what happens that's important, it's what you can prove in court. The written word is your most powerful weapon in court. Be sure to use it.

Pitfall #9: *Opening your mouth too wide.* If you are involved in what potentially could be a lawsuit, think before you act. Do not write offensive letters to your adversary, stating your legal positions. Successful litigation involves some element of surprise. State firmly but vaguely that you intend to pursue your legal remedies.

Pitfall #10: *Owning all of your assets in one business entity.* Do not place all of your eggs in one basket. While a corporation or a limited liability company may shield your personal assets from business liabilities, it will not shield the business's own assets. If your business entity has a substantial amount of debt-free equipment or Real Estate, consider spreading out the risk. Create one or more corporations or limited partnerships to hold the title to the asset, then have your business lease the assets back.

John D Rockefeller once said, own nothing, but control everything. The more assets your business owns, the more likely it will be sued. Whatever business you are in, look deep to see where your risk is.

For instance, let's say you have a business that deals with the public. That's one area that can be separated and protected by forming one corporation. Let's also assume that there is equipment you have that you want to protect. And maybe you have a building that you operate your business from. These assets can be leased from your other corporation. You can end up in a scenario where you might have the employees in one corporation, leasing their services to the main company that deals with the public. In turn, that organization really doesn't have any assets in it, but the assets it uses are held in a third company that leases these assets such as the tools or a building the main operating company owns. So, say a group of people sues the main operating company because they are not happy with the work that was performed and they find there is nothing to take from the main operating company or if one of the employees sues his or her employer, all the employer has is a corporation that just has employees and no assets in it. You want to think of how to structure yourself in this way.

Nevada corporations offer a high degree of privacy. In most states, when you set up a business structure, you file your form with the state to set up that business structure and you get the information back from the state that asks for the ownership. Who the owners are, what ownership percentages they have over the business, where they are located, and what their Social Security numbers are all kept in state databases and easily obtained by anyone who gets into those databases to check the information. Nevada has come to be known as "the privacy state." Nevada does not archive or collect a lot of data on business structures that are set up. One of the unique things is you don't have to live in Nevada to set up a business structure. You can literally live anywhere you want to in the world, and have a business structure formed and operated that you run, manage, and control that was set up, on paper, in Nevada. Again, you are not doing this to dodge ex-spouses or run from creditors. You are doing this legally for completely lawful purposes.

There are other advantages about Nevada corporations. For instance, you can have "bearer shares," which means that the owners of the corporations do not have to disclose their ownership. And they hold the stock certificate in "bearer forms" where on the face of the certificate, it simply states "bearer." In this case, it's like a stock certificate that is just owned by the holder, the person who actually has it in his or her possession.

For example, what if you are living in another state and you want to own and control a corporation? You have a McDonald's franchise in Utah and you are operating that business day in and day out, but you don't really want your ownership there. You can have a separate Nevada corporation on the stock of this business. You are still operating the business and you don't give up control, but you've achieved some financial privacy because your name is not being publicly listed on the records. Always be aware that you want to give out the least amount of personal data and personal information. If you can take advantage of not having mail go to your physical address, use a post office box or some alternate address. Maybe it's at your office. Everyone knows that you are at your office, and that you work there day in and day out. Have all your personal mail directed there.

Seize every opportunity to maintain privacy in your life. The less you show up on public records, the less likely that litigation and lawsuits will be filed against you.

How about your retirement funds? You want to think about ways of protecting your financial assets. One of the things you can do to protect those assets and achieve some privacy in your life is, for instance, on investments you might have, such as insurance products. Investment products brought under the umbrella of an insurance company are credible proof, and it's the same with any kind of retirement programs or profit sharing programs that you set up for your business such as IRAs, SEP plans, and any kind of 401(k) program that you might have in your business. It's important to understand that these are all creditor protected. Both state and federal governments help protect you, in that, if you have set aside money for your retirement, it's protected from litigation. So, if you've got money sitting in a bank account, think about putting it into a retirement plan that will help shield it.

This book is all about creating wealth in your life. But you've also got to think about how you are going to preserve that wealth. And wealth creation leads right into wealth preservation. You need to create strategies that lower your profile and protect yourself from creditors and from litigation that might come your way.

You don't want to retire and find out that the money you have amassed and the Real Estate you have is all of a sudden going to be taken from you because of some problem that occurred in your life. Something could happen. Maybe it's an accident that the court finds you personally responsible for. All of a sudden, it could cost you millions of dollars, and even the insurance that's available to protect you is often not enough to truly protect you.

Let's review everything we've talked about in this chapter.

So What?

We've talked about financial privacy and the need for it. It comes down to things that are taking place such as identity theft, and the explosion of lawsuits that can come out of nowhere. Lowering your profile and using the appropriate corporate structure is the answer.

Do you buy everything you have with credit cards so that there is a profile about you on your credit card? Yes, you can get travel points and other advantages from credit cards. But think about the fact that you're giving up financial privacy where anybody can pull a profile on you and find out where you shop, where you eat, and how much money you spend. Searchers can identify probably how much you make from that information, too, simply by gaining access to your credit card information. Those same credit card companies now sell information about you to marketing firms, so those marketing firms can identify what kind of information to send you in the mail or what kind of information to sell the telemarketing firms that call your house or spammers who send you messages on the Internet. That same information is available to anybody who is trying to sue you, who wants to develop a personal profile on you before going to court and deciding whether or not to proceed or not.

Think about how you've structured your life. Think about what your profile looks like. Think about how much money you are spending and how you are spending it. Think about how flashy your lifestyle is. To eliminate risks from lawsuits, just keep a lower profile—a lower, existence. Don't just volunteer information about yourself. Anytime you are completing medical forms, forms at stores you are buying products from, don't give them all the information. You have no obligation.

For example, when you go into a store and are asked about your personal address so that they can search your file, don't give them your actual physical address, use a post office box. Achieve some financial privacy. And again it comes down to this: own nothing, control everything. And you've got the ultimate fortress created for yourself where maybe all your assets are all set up in a trust for your children's benefit. They are not yours anymore and they are protected in those trusts. Think about the financial investments you have. Consider the asset protection advantages of investment products offered by insurance companies.

Protecting your financial privacy protects you from financial crime and helps keep money in your pocket, where it belongs.

CHAPTER 9
Reducing Taxes

Matthew 22:17-22 "*17 Tell us therefore, What thinkest thou? Is it lawful to give tribute unto Caesar, or not? 18 But Jesus perceived their wickedness, and said, Why tempt ye me, ye hypocrites? 19 Shew me the tribute money. And they brought unto him a penny. 20 And he saith unto them, Whose is this image and superscription? 21 They say unto him, Caesar's. Then saith he unto them, Render therefore unto Caesar the things which are Caesar's; and unto God the things that are God's. 22 When they had heard these words, they marveled, and left him, and went their way.*"

In this chapter, we will talk about the ways that you, as an entrepreneur, can reduce the many types of taxes that you pay. This includes everything from business and personal taxes to probate fees. When the word "taxes" is mentioned to some entrepreneurs, they almost immediately want to skip over the topic and get to "the good stuff." "Teach me something that makes me money," they will say. But it is important for you to stop and think more about this.

Every dollar you save in taxes is a dollar more in your pocket. The bottom line is what you should think about. If it makes, saves, or preserves your wealth, you should spend some time studying it. That's what this chapter is all about. It's no wonder that people shy away from even thinking about taxes. Here is a test for you. Who said, "The hardest thing in the world to understand is the income tax?" The answer is Albert Einstein. He is also thought to have remarked, when confronted with a Form 1040 personal income tax return, "I am a mathematician, not a philosopher."

The tax situation keeps changing and getting more complicated. "Since the beginning of 2001, there have been more than 3,250 changes to the tax code, an average of more than one a day, including more than 500 changes in 2008 alone.

"The Code has grown so long that it has become challenging even to figure out how long it is. A search of the Code conducted in the course of preparing this report turned up 3.7 million words.

"A 2001 study published by the Joint Committee on Taxation put the number of words in the Code at that time at 1,395,000.7. A 2005 report by a tax research organization put the number of words at 2.1 million, and notably, found that the number of words in the Code has more than tripled since 1975. (NTA report.)"

The tax law took up a mere thirty-one pages back then. As of 2004, it had grown into a whopping 60,044 pages—a twenty-five-volume beast and it keeps getting bigger and more convoluted each year. According to the tax foundation, the typical middle-income taxpayer in 2012 had to work until April 19 just to cover his or her federal and state income taxes. That's almost a third of the year, amounting to one hundred and nine days or out of each eight-hour day, two hours and twenty-three minutes worth of earnings. In comparison, in 1930 taxes took only thirty seconds of each eight-hour day. With almost six hundred different tax forms to deal with, we collectively spend 5.4 billion hours a year filling out IRS paperwork.

An economist of the University of Michigan estimates that just managing our income taxes cost us more than $115,000,000,000 a year. That's even more than what the federal government spends on education, homeland security, and an economist of the University of Michigan state combined..

There's no doubt that taxes consume too much of our income. The average American now spends more time working to pay his taxes than he or she does working to provide food, clothing, and shelter. Sit down to do your taxes and you find the instructions more complex than ever. The short form, Form 1040A, now has more than eighty pages of instructions and twice the number of lines that appeared in the standard full-blown Form 1040 back in 1945. So much for tax simplification.

And good luck getting any help from the IRS. The information the IRS offers taxpayers is often wrong. The treasury inspector general for tax administration reported that taxpayers received incorrect or no answers to 43 percent of tax questions asked in a special study. The investigators concluded that a total of about 500,000 taxpayers who visited IRS help centers got wrong or incomplete responses. The very problems people try to solve often end up getting worse once the IRS gets involved.

For example, the 2003 changes in taxes on dividend and capital gains have resulted in a disaster. The IRS has estimated that it takes almost eight hours for the average taxpayer to compete a schedule D. This is the section you fill out if you sold out any capital asset such as stocks or mutual funds or if you received any dividends qualifying for the lower rate. If you fill out the whole return—Form 1040 and Schedules A, B, C, D, and E—you're looking at forty-four hours of work if you do it yourself, spending fourteen hours on the 1040 alone. And the IRS says the Form 1040EZ will take three and a half hours. Even audits aren't handled correctly. The IRS audit rate for 2012 was 29.3 percent up from .57 percent in 2002. However, the percentage of no change audits has grown from 14 percent in fiscal 2001 to 62 percent in 2012, a significant increase and a waste of time and resources.

Why is the IRS auditing the wrong people? Well, for one thing, their formulas for selecting returns are way out of date. The formulas do things like compare your income and zip code with average deductions for that area income class. A return claiming a big charitable deduction by someone who lives in a lower income zip code might generate a computer flag. The more flags a return generates, the higher the chances the return will be kicked out of the system for human review. So what can you do to prevent it?

I'll start with using the tax code for your own gain. While filling out your taxes is tedious, it also provides you with an opportunity to look back on what you did right and wrong in the past year and learn from it. Granted, Monday morning quarterbacking won't change the game but financial hindsight can certainly help you plan for a better, smarter tax year in the coming year.

Here's an example: If you are not creating quarterly financial reports, and a lot of smaller businesses don't, then going over your schedule C may be the only time you'll look at your businesses' financial results. This section tells you where your expenses are going and then you can decide whether your business is overspending in one category and perhaps not spending enough than another.

Let's look at the information for audit rates. Right now, one of the highest audit rates happens with individuals running a small business, whether it's home based or a small shop. A self-employed individual who uses a legal structure like a corporation or a limited liability company has the highest audit rate. These individuals run a business under their own name as a sole proprietorship either with or without employees. Right now, sole proprietorships is the highest audited category in our country. The second highest audited category is with partnerships. Anybody who is involved in a general partnership with two or more parties should be aware that the category of partnerships has an almost 10 percent audit rate. That means, one in ten people in partnerships are being audited each year.

One of the best areas in which to position yourself for any type of business is a small corporation—one that you run. The current audit rate on small corporations is only about 1 percent. That's a very low number. Keep these audit numbers in mind when you're determining the company structure that's right for you.

One of the best ways of saving money on your taxes is by avoiding the most common tax mistakes that people make. According to the Internal Revenue Service, errors in addition and subtraction are the number one mistake made by taxpayers. All returns are examined for mathematical errors. Mistakes in arithmetic or in transferring figures from one schedule to another result in an immediate correction notice. If the error leads to a tax deficiency, you automatically receive a bill for that amount. If you overpaid, the excess is applied to future taxes and credited or refunded at your request. You can appeal such corrections and you can make a written request asking that they be reviewed if the IRS made a mistake. Also, check the figures on the

IRS correction notice. They've been known to make mistakes, too. Math mistakes alone rarely lead to a full audit.

Another common error is forgetting about dividend and interest payment. Dividend and interest payments are reported to the IRS by banks' brokerage houses and other financial institutions and are cross-checked in about 96 percent of cases. The IRS attempts to match almost a 100 percent of the returns they receive electronically or on computer tape and more than 50 percent of those they receive on paper. As a result of this cross-checking, the IRS sends out notices for taxes and interest on overdue taxes for income and other payments that were not reported. Unfortunately, according to the U.S. The U.S. General Accounting Office was renamed the U.S. General Accountability Office in 2004 (the government agency that audits for the IRS), about half of the ten million correction notices the IRS issued in 2012 were incorrect, unresponsive, unclear, or incomplete.

If you get an Incorrect Notice, follow the appropriate procedures to contest it or contact your local problem resolution office.

Another common problem is not properly tracking an investment basis. A basis is the original value of your investment. If you have mutual funds, for example, each year those funds will report the dividends and capital gains you've earned. These dividends and gains will be taxable when you were reporting. When you sell these funds, your gain will be the difference between what you receive on the sale and your basis. Technically, your amount realized last year adjusted the initial investment basis. The basis increases once any financial gain you reinvested are taxed. If you re-invested, taxable gains from these funds and all the dividends and capital gains reported are added to your basis to reduce your gain or increase your loss.

For example, if I bought a fund for $1,000 and re-invested $200 in dividends and $50 in capital gains, my basis is now $1250. If I sell the fund for $1500, I only have to recognize $250 in gain on that sale. That's much better than reporting a $500 profit for tax purposes. To make sure you have the right basis, check with your fund company (investment company) or broker. If you can't get the data by the April 15 filing deadline, you can either file for an extension or file an amended return later.

Another big problem, especially for small businesses, is losing track of receipts. Always keep your receipts and checks if you want to deduct them. Always keep deductible receipts and checks for at least three years from the due date of the year filed or, if you're filing later, keep them from the actual date filed. Unless the IRS can prove fraud, the statute of limitations to disallow deductions is three years. Once this three-year-period has elapsed, the IRS is prohibited from even questioning these deductions. Receipts for expenses that may be deducted in later years, such as improvement to your house, should be kept for three years after the return on which they're claimed.

Remember, the IRS is a paper-based bureaucracy. Separate your receipts and checks by deductible category and make any audit easier for the auditor. The easier you make it for him or her, the more the auditor will believe and accept the premise that you know what you're doing and will therefore make it easier on you.

To help you meet the records requirement of the IRS, whether as a corporation or as a sole proprietorship, you need three separate and distinct tax records: permanent files, regular files, and a daily journal. Regardless of how you conduct your business, whether as a corporation or as a sole proprietorship, you need three separate and distinct tax records: permanent files, regular files, and a daily diary.

Your permanent files include your prior year's tax returns, stock purchases and sales, equipment purchases and sales, and similar entries. Generally, you want to keep any record that relates to more than one year in your permanent file. If you purchased property, your permanent file should include the purchase document, closing statements, deed, and other expenses related to the purchase. Include your prior year's tax returns, stock purchases and sales, equipment purchases, and sales in similar entries. Generally, you want to keep any record that relates to more than one tax year in your permanent file.

The second section is your regular file. These files include time sheets for part-time help, receipts, invoices, canceled checks, and other corroborative evidence.

Finally, there's your daily diary. Your daily diary, which can be your appointment book, is the focal point of your documentation system. This is especially true if you operate a personal service business. The smaller your business, the more important this document becomes. Your daily diary should include: All of your appointments, where and when you travel, where you go by car, and where and when you entertained your business contact. A second strategy is to keep a separate business checkbook and use three-part checks.

Regardless of your business form, whether a corporation or sole proprietorship, three-part checking is necessary to build good, easy-to-use records in your regular files. Send part one, the original of the check to the vendor. Staple supporting evidence such as receipts or invoices to part two of the check, and file alphabetically in the vendor file. Finally, put part three of the check in the numerical file for later viewing by IRS and reference by you.

The third strategy is to keep Form 1099 information separate. Negligence penalties are automatic if you fail to report all of the income that's reported to the IRS on Form 1099. The negligence penalty applies to your total underpayment of tax, not just the portion due to negligence. Any deposits that you make that would normally not be included in the 1099 or W2 should be copied. Thus, if you get a large gift, insurance reimbursement, or if you transfer money from one account to another, make copies of the checks. Failure to do so may result in the IRS treating the deposit as income. And that strategy is to save every receipt, whether personal or business, for all money spent. It's virtually impossible for you to know all of the receipts you're required to keep. Since you don't know what's important and what's not, it's safest to save everything for at least three years. Remember, you carry the burden of proof. It's rare that you can establish proof retroactively.

The final strategy is to use a business credit card. To keep your record-keeping burden to a minimum, use a separate charge card for all your business expenditures. By using one or more credit cards solely for business, you can deduct the finance charges on the business card as well as the annual fees on all cards used solely for business.

Here's another tax hint: Group or bunch your deductions. There are a number of deductions that are allowed only after you exceed a minimum amount. For example, only medical expenses that exceed 7.5 percent of your adjusted gross income are allowed. Alternatively, miscellaneous deductions are allowed only to the extent that they exceed 2 percent of your adjusted gross income. Your best planning strategy here is to bunch your deductions into a single year to exceed this minimum requirement.

For example, if you have an adjusted gross income of a $100,000, only those medical expenses in excess of $7,500 can be deducted. In order to exceed this floor amount, you might re-pay your dental bill or pay your January first medical insurance on December 31. With miscellaneous itemized deductions and the same adjusted gross income, you need to exceed $2,000 in expenses.

In addition, there are some tips that just apply to the business that you run. For example, many small business owners vastly underestimate the mileage they spend driving to the bank, going to meetings, getting supplies, and anything else that applies to their particular business. If you are in this category, go back through your day-timer for the year and figure out your mileage. It may astound you how many miles you actually drove. Beginning January 1, 2014, the standard mileage deduction is 56 cents per mile for business miles driven or you can use the actual expense method, which is a bit of a pain to keep track of. For a few years now, you have been allowed to use the mileage method with leased cars. In prior years, you couldn't use the standard mileage allowance if you leased your car. Remember that miles driven from your home to work are not deductible, only miles driven from workplace to workplace.

Also, look at your meal and entertainment expenses. Expenses for meals while entertaining clients or prospective clients are subject to a 50 percent limitation. However, meals that are deemed for the convenience of the employer such as working late or working through lunch are fully deductible. Occasional meals off the business premises are also permissible under the same rule. Ask yourself this question, "Do you have a home office? Did you order pizza while working late?" Let your employer—your business corporation—pay for it. This is an important distinction. If your company provides meals for its employees while working late in the office, it's a 100 percent deduction, not 50 percent. Do you work at home? Can you bear eating at your desk? Be creative. Keep good records and maximize your bottom line.

Here's another tip that few people take advantage of: It's known as IRC section 179. This provision of the code allows you to expense rather than depreciate certain capital assets such as computers, cell phones, and other equipment. Thus, you can fully deduct the cost of these items you purchased in the year rather than depreciate them over several years. You cannot deduct these items to create a loss but you can carry the unused expenses forward to the next year.

These are strategies you can use right now to start saving money on your taxes. (For more information, see http://www.section179.org/index.html.)

Now let's step back a bit and look at some of the long-range tax planning that you can do for your business. The first thing is to look at the tax benefit associated with the C corporation. A C corporation is a tax shelter that provides many benefits for the small business entrepreneur. A C corporation can provide tax-free financial planning and income tax preparation help to employees. It can also establish a medical insurance and medical reimbursement plan for its shareholder employees.

The cost of medical and dental insurance premiums and deductibles can be paid by the corporation and fully deducted. The benefit is not taxable to the employee. To be tax-free, such benefits must be part of a written employee benefit plan and available to all employees, not just the owners. If you and your spouse are the only employees, is this a problem? Of course not.

A C corporation can provide employees with group life insurance coverage and deduct the premium costs. Only group term life insurance qualifies. Death proceeds for beneficiaries are limited to $50,000 for each employee. If greater coverage is provided, the cost is still deductible to the corporation. But the cost of the additional coverage is taxable to the employee as income. A C corporation's shareholder can borrow up to $10,000 from the corporation interest free. The loans still must be documented but the IRS will not impute interest. This is an ideal way to take out money without the double tax issue. A C corporation's income is taxed at the corporate level and then again at the shareholder level, but only when dividends are distributed. Finally, a C corporation can set up a profit-sharing plan for its employees. The shareholder employee of such a plan can actually borrow out of the plan. Properly utilized, this strategy can provide excellent opportunities for the entrepreneur.

For another tax strategy for your business, you should become familiar with the three types of income and how they're taxed at the corporate level.

1. *Earned income.* Money earned through a trade or business.
2. *Portfolio income.* Money earned by monetary investment such as stocks and bonds. Examples would be interest, dividends, and capital gains. And finally,
3. *Passive income.* Income that investments earn. A company could earn income such as a small business that is incorporated as a limited liability company.

Unless the LLC has elected different tax treatment, a single-member LLC will be taxed just like a sole proprietorship, and a multimember LLC will be taxed as a general partnership. That means the owners of an LLC will be subject to a self-employment tax of 15.3 percent for earned income. A company could also have portfolio income derived from interest, dividends, and capital gains. If you set up a C corporation to own assets that appreciate and then later sell them for gain, the corporation will have capital gains. The corporation will also have a major problem because C corporations do not get the special capital gains treatment that individuals do. A company could also have passive income. Generally, passive income is associated with an appreciating asset. You generally do not want to have a C corporation on Real Estate due to the unfavorable tax consequences that result.

So what is the best structure from a tax point of view? To fully answer that question, you will need to know how much money you expect to make from this venture. What type of money will you make? If you formed a C corporation, what tax-free benefits could you take? Will you build depreciating assets within the company? What is your exit strategy? What funding requirements will your business have? How will you raise the money for your business and will you need to bring in a partner? If so, what will their role be?

For example, let's say you're buying or selling stock. One of the best ways of reducing your taxes is to avoid running it through your personal tax return because you're paying the highest taxes on that return. Use an entity like a corporation or a limited partnership or a limited liability company.

Let's look at another type of tax that most people forget about: sales taxes. What are some of the strategies that can help you reduce the amount of taxes you pay in sales taxes? In many cases, you reduce sales taxes if you purchase online and if the online store that you're buying from is in another state. Depending on your state sales tax legislation, you can often eliminate sales taxes on those purchases. What if you need a computer for the kids at home? Purchase it online from a service that can ship it directly to your house, eliminating some of those sales taxes which can really add up. Sales taxes can range anywhere from 5 to 10 percent in some states and cities. Eliminating those sales taxes can be a tremendous benefit to the bottom line of your personal financial situation. Aside from online shopping, look at states like Delaware that don't have any sales tax. Figure out how you can purchase any larger items in states like this.

Let's look at estate planning now. Estate taxes are paid by our heirs. Ultimately when we pass away, the estate taxes are paid to the IRS and can be as high as 65 percent of the value of our estate.

One of the things you should explore is a family limited partnership. Family limited partnerships allow you to take your personal and business assets and put them into an entity. This is a legal structure in which your children or your heirs become the owners of those assets but you, as the parents, are still controlling the assets. A major concern that people have is that their children could mismanage their financial affairs. With a family limited partnership, the parents control those assets until they die.

There are some wonderful things you can do with insurance today to reduce the amount you have to pay in estate taxes. Again, this is where you need a strategy developed. You want to sit down with an estate planner who is going to design the strategy to reduce those taxes that will be paid upon your death. It's simplifying the process for your children because you want your children to hang on to everything you worked so hard for and not have it go to the Internal Revenue Service. Planning and laying out some structures to reduce those potential taxes, investigating insurance alternatives, and getting your assets into your children's names prior to your death is what you need to do.

Before I leave estate planning ideas, let's talk about probate. Probate, lawyers say, is simply a safeguard designed to ensure that your wishes are honored and your family protected when you are no longer around to oversee matters yourself. An impartial court supervises the whole process to look out for the interest of both your family and your creditors. What's wrong with that? A lot, unfortunately. Probate costs a considerable amount of money. The fees vary widely from state to state. A probate attorney, court, and other expenses often eat up about 5 percent or more of the value of property left behind at death. As a result, that much less goes to the people or charities you wanted it to reach. If the estate is complicated or disputed, the fees can be even larger. Probate costs might be justified if the process really did something for families but in most instances, there is no conflict so there is no need to be in court.

For example, a man leaves a will with everything going to his widow and children. This is pretty common. No one is challenging the validity of the will and the family is willing to pay whatever bills he left and divide the property according to his wishes. Why have a lengthy court proceeding? Formal notification of relatives and creditors and extensive publication of death notices is in the legal notices column of a newspaper. The property merely needs to be handed over to the new owners, which is what probate avoidance methods let you do.

Probate is such a profit center for lawyers that they'll go to great lengths to secure this business. The probate windfall explains why lawyers usually charge less for wills than for other documents of comparable complexity. They are hoping to cash in later when the will must be probated. It's no exaggeration to say that many lawyers plan for their later years by anticipating lucrative probate cases regularly coming their way.

A lawyer who accepts a probate case is almost guaranteed a nice profit for little effort. Generally, probate entails lots of tedious paperwork but minimal or no original work. There are few court appearances, if any, and rarely are lawyers called upon to craft a legal argument or conduct anything resembling a trial. Lawyers' fees are set by statute or local custom and often bear no relation to actual work done. Courts are supposed to keep an eye on fees but in practice, they seldom intervene. And lawyers are usually paid first before the beneficiaries.

Probate also takes a long time, often up to a year, during which time the beneficiaries generally get nothing unless the judge allows the immediate family a family allowance. In some states, this is a pittance—only a few hundred dollars. In others, it can amount to thousands. In any case, the family is forced to ask a court for use of its own money. Delay can be more than an annoyance. It can cost major life disruptions. A student about to enter college may not be able to if a parent's assets are tied up in probate for months or years. A surviving spouse may not be able to move or take a new job and it is especially hard to run or sell a small business with the court looking over your shoulder.

Probate is also public. Few people ever stop to think that your will, a very personal document, which may reveal a lot about both financial and family circumstances, becomes a matter of public record after its writer dies. Like all other probate documents, wills are examined and filed and can be inspected by anyone who goes to the courthouse and asks. If, on the other hand, you arranged for your property to pass outside of probate via a living trust or payable on death bank account or life insurance vehicle, for example, the transaction is private. No documents are filed with the court or other government entity. What you leave to whom, remains private. So while avoiding probate is important, at the same time, it's not a magic wand that solves every financial problem that might surface after your death.

For example, avoiding probate doesn't mean avoiding taxes. In fact, the two are completely unrelated. Another matter that working outside of probate doesn't change is your family's right to inherit. If you're married, your spouse has a right to some of the property you leave at your death. And using probate avoidance techniques to transfer the property doesn't change that. This, of course, is not a problem for most people. Most of us want to pass on whatever wealth we've accumulated to our spouses and children.

In case you're concerned about this issue, however, here are the general rules regarding your family's rights. Many married people leave most, if not all of their property to their spouses. If you don't, your spouse may have the right to go to court and claim some of your property after your death. The rights of spouses vary from state to state. In the community property states, Arizona, California, Idaho, Louisiana, Nevada, New Mexico, Texas, Washington, and Wisconsin, the general rule is that spouses together own all property that either acquires during the marriage except property one spouse receives by gift or inheritance. Each spouse owns a half interest in this community property. You're free to leave your separate property and your half of the community property to anyone you choose. In all other states, a surviving spouse who doesn't receive at least one third to one half of the deceased spouse's property through a will, living trust, or other method, is entitled to insist upon that amount. The exact share depends on state law. In short, a spouse who doesn't receive the minimum he or she is entitled to under state law, the statutory share, may be entitled to some of the property in your living trust. Don't try to cut out your spouse. If you don't plan to leave at least half of the property in your estate to your spouse, you should consult a lawyer experienced in estate planning.

State law may also give your spouse the right to inherit the family residence. The Florida Constitution, for example, gives a surviving spouse the family residence. The spouse is free, of course, to voluntarily give up this right.

Probate also doesn't affect what you leave your children. Although most children inherit the bulk of their parents' property, usually after both parents have died, it isn't mandated by law. Put bluntly, you don't have to leave your children anything. The law protects only children who appear to have been accidentally overlooked—

typically, children born after the parent's will was signed. Such children are entitled to a share determined by state law of the deceased parent's estate, which may include property in a living trust. So if you don't want to leave any property to one or more of your children—perhaps they have plenty of money or you've already given them their inheritances—make a will and mention each child in it. And to avoid any later misunderstandings or hurt feelings, explain your actions to your children either in your will or better yet, while you're still around. Grandchildren have no right to inherit from their grandparents unless their parent has died. In that case, the grandchildren essentially take the place of the deceased child and are entitled to whatever he or she would have been legally entitled to.

Finally, avoiding probate doesn't let you off the hook from legal obligations to your creditors. If you don't leave enough to pay your debts and taxes, any assets that pass outside of probate may be subject to the claims of creditors after your death. If there is any probate proceeding, your executor—the person named in your will to handle your affairs your death—can demand that whoever inherited the property turn over some of it or all of it so creditors can be paid. Creditors, however, only have a set amount of time, about three to six months in most states, to submit formal claims to your executor. A creditor who is properly notified of the probate court proceeding cannot file a claim after the deadline passes.

On the other hand, when property isn't probated, creditors' claims aren't cut off so quickly. In theory at least, a creditor could track down the property and sue the new owner to collect the debt a year or two later. As a practical matter, however, avoiding probate may actually provide more protection from creditors. When property is distributed without probate, there is no legal requirement as there is in probate that creditors be notified in writing. They may not know of the death for years. They may not know where the property went, especially if the debt is small. It may not be worth their while to track down the new owners and try to collect. Most people don't need to worry that after their death, creditors will line up to collect large debts from the estate. In most situations, the surviving relatives simply pay the valid debts such as monthly bills, taxes, and medical and funeral expenses. But if you're concerned about the possibility of large claims, you may want to let your property go through probate.

Given all the drawbacks of probate, it's not surprising that people have sought ways around it. In a nutshell, you can avoid probate by using other documents in place of a will or by transferring property before your death such as setting up a payable-on-death bank account or naming a beneficiary for your retirement accounts, your stocks and bonds or holding property in joint ownership.

Forty years ago, almost the only way to avoid probate was by using a trust. New methods have come along as part of new government-created types of investments such as private retirement accounts. Doing some planning so that your family will be spared the red tape and expense after your death is sensible. But keep in mind that probate doesn't happen until after your death. If you're young and healthy, a will that lets you leave property to the people you choose and name someone you want to raise your children, if you have any, is probably all the estate planning you need. You can worry about probate later.

In other words, use common sense. As you get older and decide it's worthwhile to do some probate avoidance planning, keep in mind that your family will reap the most benefits if your big ticket possessions like Real Estate and large bank or investment accounts don't go through probate.

So What?

Let's review what we have learned in this chapter. We've explored the ways that saving money on your taxes can definitely add to your bottom line. Keeping the right records may seem like a burden when you are keeping track of small pieces of paper and files throughout the year, but these savings can pay off big time. This is true whether they are federal taxes, personal taxes, sales taxes, or estate taxes, including probate fees. Choosing the right corporate structure can also reduce your taxes and lower your chances of an audit.

The chapters so far in this book have discussed the ways of starting and building your own business can provide for your current needs while your business can also help you meet your retirement needs in the future.

CHAPTER 10
Planning Your Retirement

Proverbs 16:1-3 *"16 The preparations of the heart in man, and the answer of the tongue, is from the Lord. 2 All the ways of a man are clean in his own eyes; but the Lord weigheth the spirits. 3 Commit thy works unto the Lord, and thy thoughts shall be established."*

In this chapter of the book, I am going to talk about your retirement and what it all means for your financial and business plans. I'll be talking about some new insurance products that are available for your use in your business as well as the various pension and benefit plans that your company can set up for your retirement benefit.

Many entrepreneurs have ideas about retirement that are a little out of date. They might believe, for example, that there's always plenty of time to think about planning for their retirement. Alternatively they might believe that the government, through Social Security, might be all that they need to meet their retirement needs for a few years of retirement but, in reality, things are different today.

Today life expectancy is increasing dramatically. Living to age one hundred is no longer news. Retirement has been transformed from a handful of quiet years into an active, healthy third life that stretches twenty, thirty, or more years into the future. Well, this is good news. But it presents a real problem for those who fail to plan ahead as retirement life ends. Outliving your money becomes a practical concern to ensure financial security and independent living. For those decades, your financial planning goals must take these changes into consideration. The financial world is also moving away from a picture where retirees could count on Social Security and their pension plan providing for all their retirement needs. Social Security is constantly being tinkered with by politicians. First we hear about how the program is going broke, the next minute it's fixed and will be going broke in 2020 or 2030. The bottom line is that no matter what politician you believe, Social Security benefits aren't going to increase in the future. At best they will stay where they are today, which means that you'll have to do some retirement planning to make up the difference. In terms of private pension plans, fewer and fewer people in the United States have them.

The days when you would work for thirty or thirty-five years with one company and then retire for ten or fifteen years with the company paying benefits to you are long gone. People today change employers far more often and employers are going bankrupt as well as threatening any long-term pension payouts. If you're an entrepreneur running your own business there are no parent companies setting up a pension for you when you retire, unless you set up a plan in your company. (I'll talk about that in detail later on this chapter.) There will be no pot of money for you to fund your retirement needs.

All of this may sound intimidating, but it shouldn't be. I am here to help you determine what your financial needs at your retirement are going to be and then give you solid strategies to meet those needs.

The first strategy is that no matter what your age, you and your company should start saving for the future. Because of the power of compounding, the sooner you start saving and putting money away the better off you're going to be in the long run. Once you've reached the point when your business is on solid ground, that's the time to get started saving.

There are several types of pension plans available to owners of corporations of any size and these plans have unique benefits in both tax savings and wealth accumulation. You can maximize the power of tax deferral, get higher returns on your investments, and leverage your investments for even greater returns. You can also borrow from your investments. Best of all, you have complete control of your money. Pension plans are safe from creditors and judgments. In addition, these benefit plans are also good for your company. They produce incentives to encourage key employees to remain loyal to you, therefore reducing employee turnover. The plan your company sets up is two-pronged: tax deferral and the power of compounding. Harnessing the power of tax-deferred income combined with compound interest can multiply your retirement income significantly.

For instance, if your goal is to retire in thirty years with a million dollars, it would take a monthly investment of $1,644 and an annual return of 5 percent, assuming a tax rate of 35 percent. Increasing the returns to 12 percent results in a monthly payment of $699, but if you had a 12 percent rate of return with all taxes deferred until withdrawn at retirement, it would only require a monthly investment of $286 to grow to a million dollars in thirty years.

Before we look at the specifics, let's make a distinction between what we'll call a qualified plan and a non-qualified plan. A qualified plan simply means that your contributions are tax deductible. There is a tax deduction either to the individual or to the corporation, depending on the type of plan it is. A non-qualified plan, which we'll get to in a moment, means that there is no immediate tax deduction. In order to understand the rules related to qualified plans, you need to step back and look at the big picture.

All tax-qualified retirement plans such as pension and profit-sharing plans, including 401(k) plans, are subject to the massive pension loan known as the Employee Retirement Income Security Act of 1974 or ERISA. ERISA offers employers a trade off. You can go ahead and set up a tax-sheltered retirement plan but if you do, you have to protect your rank and file employees. This means there's a minimum standard for covering employees and a minimum contribution you have to make for them.

There's also a fiduciary standard. It requires you to protect the assets set aside for your employees' retirement.

Let's look at the tax advantage plans that are available to you through your company. The first type of qualified plan available is a SEPP (Simplified Employee Pension Plan). A SEPP plan can be set up for a one-person corporation or sole proprietorship. Essentially, an employer sets up an account and makes contributions. These funds can be invested in a variety of investment vehicles, including mutual funds and money market accounts and other investments. Annual contributions are limited to 25 percent of the owner's compensation or $51,000, whichever is lower. All contributions are deductible to the corporation. A SEPP program is simple to set up and simple to administer. A SEPP plan is also protected from creditors.

Another type of plan is the familiar 401(k) plan. A 401(k) plan allows for deferral of income tax based on a percentage of salary. The first step in determining if a 401(k) plan would be right for your business is to complete a company census and have that documented and analyzed by a competent actuary or pension plan administrator or firm. The U.S. House recently voted to raise the limits on IRAs and 401(k) plans. Currently, the maximum 2013 annual pretax contributions to a 401(k) plan is $17,500. Also the amount of annual pay on which total contributions are based on is from $178,000 to $188,000. All 401(k) plans are subject to complex IRS rules and total compliance can be difficult. There is also significant cost to setting up and administering the plan. Because of these issues, this type of plan isn't recommended for small companies or corporations.

Instead of a traditional 401(k) plan, you should consider what is known as a simple 401(k) plan. This type is similar to a 401(k) plan but would lower administration and set up cost. Many of the compliance issues with a regular 401(k) are not required with the simple 401(k) plan. This works well for small companies with one or two highly compensated individuals or owners.

A plan with many advantages is known as a defined benefit plan. Defined benefit plans are the most advantageous for individuals who want to retire within seven to fifteen years and who have a significant amount of money to contribute. All contributions are tax deferred and are treated as a corporate expense. Defined benefit plans are set up to provide monthly benefits at retirement age depending on the amount of the contribution, anticipated rate of growth, and years of service with the company. An actuary determines the contributions required to meet the goals of the plan. Defined benefit plans provide the greatest opportunity for contributions and deductions. If the plan is established when the owners are forty or older, the benefits can be much larger than other types of plans. Defined benefit plans are more difficult to set up and require a professional administrator, but there are several variations on defined benefit plans. Additional benefits include the ability to contribute up to $10,000 on behalf of non-compensated family members, and loans of up to $50,000 against the plan are also allowed.

Owners of defined benefit plans must file form 5500 with the IRS and operate under a letter of approval, reviewed and submitted by an actuary. Defined contribution plans are yet another type of plan available to you, the small business owner.

Defined contribution plans do not promise specific future payments. Instead, they're calculated by a fixed contribution based on a percentage of compensation. Defined contribution plans can be profit-sharing, money-purchase, or Employee Stock Ownership Plans known as ESOP. Contributions for all these plans are limited to $30,000 per employee or individual.

Profit-sharing plans are based on company profits and a percentage of an employee's compensation. The plan can require employees to become vested before they are eligible to collect any benefits from the plan.

Money-purchase plans are similar to profit-sharing plans with one exception. They require a minimum fixed funding amount that cannot be easily changed or adjusted. The maximum contribution is 25 percent of compensation or $30,000 per year, whichever is lower.

Employee Stock Ownership Plans (ESOPS) require fixed contributions that are invested in the stock of the company on behalf of the employees.

No matter what type of qualified plan you have, remember that these funds are protected from creditors. One of the most powerful reasons you'd want to set up your own pension plan within your business entity, either corporation or LLC, is to have creditor protection. For everything, other than an IRA, you have a 100 percent creditor protection. The one exception is that the IRS can make a levy on these plans against any taxes that are owed. Keeping this exception in mind, no matter what happens to the corporation the money you save, even if the company goes bankrupt, can't be touched because essentially the retirement money is the individual's money not the company's. Once you transfer this money from your business and take the deduction into your account, it's still off limits to creditors.

Now, let's look at non-qualified plans. Since a qualified plan is tax deductible, typically a non-qualified plan means that a contribution is not tax deductible. However, non-qualified plans don't have contributions limited in the same way that qualified plans do. Here's another plus. These plans have no matching requirements. In other words, in a non-qualified plan you're not required to match any employees or people who have been with you as employees.

Typically non-qualified plans involve some type of insurance product. They're to make sure you end up with some money for your retirement regardless of what happens in the stock market or wherever you place your money.

The main type of non-qualified plan available is called split-dollar insurance, which refers not to a type of policy but to a method of paying for a policy. In a split-dollar arrangement, the employer and employee agree to split the cost, premiums and benefits, cash value, and death benefits of a permanent life insurance policy. This agreement can take many forms. Here are the elements found in split dollar agreements.

Policy ownership. There are two basic forms of policy ownership for split-dollar policies. Endorsement method: The employer owns the policy but a written endorsement is added to the policy that splits the benefits between the employer and the employee. Collateral assignment: The employee owns the policy and assigns certain interest in this policy to the employer as collateral for payment made by the employer.

Splitting the cost of premiums. Dividing the cost of a policy can be done in any manner desired. For example, in the *classic method,* the employer pays an amount equal to the annual cash value build-up while the employee pays the balance. Another method is the *equity method*: Here, the employee pays an amount equal to the value of the economic benefit received while the employer pays the balance. In another method, the *employer pays all.* The employer pays the entire premium while the employee pays tax on the value of the economic benefit. Just as with the premium payments, the employer and employee can decide to split cash values and death benefits any way they wish.

In the *equity method,* the employer receives the total amount of the premiums paid and the employee's beneficiary receives the balance of the proceeds that pays an amount less than the amount repaid to the employer.

No matter which method you chose, there are many things you can do with a non-qualified split dollar policy.

For one thing you can use this policy as an employee fringe benefit. Since the employer can pick and chose those employees who will benefit, the split-dollar can be used to attract and retain key executives. The second advantage is the ability to use the policy for estate planning purposes. When the estate is large enough to incur a federal estate tax—taxable estate in excess of $675,000—an estate owner may consider removing life insurance from his or her estate.

A popular method of reducing death taxes is the *irrevocable life insurance trust*. Split-dollar arrangements can be used to reduce the out-of-pocket cost of the insured.

The third benefit is for business continuity purposes. In a family owned business, there is a risk of adverse tax treatment when the corporation redeems the deceased owner's stock. The proceeds of corporate-owned life insurance might also create a corporate Alternative Minimum Tax (AMT) problem. Under a corporate stock redemption, the surviving stockholders would own stock worth more but with an unchanged cost basis. These problems can be eliminated by using a cross purchase buy/sell agreement funded with life insurance. Differences between the owners in age and or percentage of ownership may cause the life insurance premiums to be expensive for some stockholders. A split-dollar arrangement may be used to assist each stockholder in purchasing enough insurance on the other stockholders.

Finally, you can consider split-dollar arrangements as a replacement for group term insurance. With the split dollar plan, the executive can have increased protection now plus substantial benefits at retirement age.

When deciding between a qualified or a non-qualified plan, consider that you should likely have a balance or a combination of the two types of plans. A qualified plan is hard to beat because of the immediate tax deduction.

Take that tax deduction and remove the money from your business entity; put it in a pension plan. Remember, many of these plans are self-directed, so you control the investments your plan makes. When you're near retirement, you should start taking that money out first because that's what will be taxed. You then let the non-qualified insurance-based product grow, tax deferred because you're going to be able to access that money tax free by having both types of plans in place, you can make maximum use of the tax laws that are in place today.

We've touched upon insurance products as part of a non-qualified retirement vehicle, but now let's look a little more closely at how an entrepreneur can use insurance wisely.

Life insurance has long been a part of estate planning in the United States. In addition to helping to support any dependents that you might have, life insurance can help solve several other common estate planning problems.

First, it provides immediate cash at death. Insurance proceeds help pay for the deceased's debts, funeral expenses, and income or death taxes. Federal estate taxes are due nine months after death, so the cash to pay for them doesn't have to be raised immediately.

By using insurance products you avoid probate. The proceeds of a life insurance policy are not subject to probate unless you name your estate as the beneficiary of the policy, which is something you definitely should not do. If anyone else, including a trust, is the beneficiary of the policy, the proceeds are not included in the probate estate and can be quickly transferred to survivors with little red tape, cost, or delay. Except when your estate has no cash ready to pay for anticipated debts and taxes, there is no sound reason for naming your estate rather than a person as the beneficiary of your life insurance policy.

Insurance also helps avoid death taxes. When an insured person does not legally own his or her life insurance policy, the proceeds are excluded from the taxable estate. This can significantly reduce death tax liability of the insured's person's estate. Obviously this is a benefit only to those whose estate is large enough to face death tax liability in the first place.

There are many sound reasons for buying life insurance but having only a single policy is not an adequate way to plan for your retirement. Most of the time, people without minor children are financially not in need of life insurance. Those who do decide to purchase insurance should know exactly why they're buying it is the best type of policy for their needs and of, course, should buy no more than they need.

Here are some questions to ask yourself when evaluating your life insurance needs. What are your long-term needs? In assessing the value of insurance that provides financial assistance to family members over the long-term, try asking yourself these questions:

How many people are really dependent on your current earning capacity over the long-term? If the answer is none, you probably don't need life insurance.

If you die suddenly, how much money would your dependents need and for how long? When you determine how much money your dependents would need, subtract the worth of the property you will leave them and any amount that would be available from public and any private insurance plans that already provide coverage. Social Security independents benefits will probably be available and you may also be covered by union or management pensions or a group life insurance plan. Don't forget to subtract any other likely sources of income such as help that grandparents might provide for your children in case of a disaster.

Once you perform this exercise, you may find that your dependents will need little or no additional income from life insurance. What are your short-term needs? Assess whether you need life insurance or short-term needs by asking yourself these questions:

After your die how long will it take your property to be turned over to your inheritors? If most of your property will avoid probate, there's usually little need for short-term insurance expenses unless you have no bank accounts, securities, or other cash assets.

By contrast, if the bulk of your property is transferred by will it would therefore be tied up in probate for months. Your family and other inheritors may need the ready cash that insurance can provide. A probate court will usually promptly authorize a family allowance or otherwise allow a spouse or another inheritor to have access to estate funds. It can still be nice to have insurance proceeds available. What other assets will be available to take care of immediate financial needs?

Aside from buying insurance, there are other cheaper ways of providing ready cash such as leaving some money in a joint or pay-on-death bank account. Also, consider placing marketable stocks and other securities in joint tenancy when you expect your estate will owe substantial debt and taxes after your death. Lawyers and financial advisors call cash and assets that can be quickly converted to cash, "liquid." If your estate has almost all no liquid assets such as Real Estate, collectables, a share in small business, there may be a significant financial loss and these assets must be sold quickly in order to raise cash for paying bills. These assets will garner greater values if sold properly in due time if there was enough liquid money from insurance or other sources to meet all pressing bills.

Obviously, if your estate has significant funds and bank accounts from marketable securities, you won't need to purchase insurance for this purpose. If you were the solo owner of a business, how much cash will your business need when you die? Do you want and expect that some of your inheritors will continue to run the business? If so, do you think there will be a significant cash flow for the new owners to successfully maintain the business? How much is your debt likely to reduce cash flow? How much will it affect the value of the business if it must be sold? Do you need insurance proceeds to cover any cash flow shortage of the business? Will there be enough cash so the business can stay alive until it is sold? Before you buy a life insurance policy, you should compare insurance rates, choose a trustworthy agent, and check the reliability of your insurance company.

After familiarizing yourself with the basic types of life insurance policies and how they can be used for retirement planning purposes, it's time to investigate cost. The cost of the same coverage can vary considerably from company to company. Often, a relatively small, mutual company charges lower rates than some of the giants seen on television advertisements; some brokers charge lower discount commissions.

To compare rates, start by visiting one of the free life insurance rate shopping reviews on the Web such a Quicken or Select Quote. Take a look at their websites which can be found at www.quicken.com and www.selectquote.com. Remember, these organizations often make money if you buy their product, which is life insurance, so only use any information they give you as a starting point. Also, a rate shopping service may offer quotes for only one type of insurance product.

Generally, you should look at various types in order to make an informed decision. Once you have a general idea of the kind of insurance you want and how much it should cost, you need to talk to an insurance salesperson or broker. Normally, a salesperson sells for one company only, while a broker can place your policy with one of many. In theory, this makes the broker look like a preferable choice but in practice, the integrity of the person you're dealing with is far more important than legal relationship to an insurance company or companies.

Although by now, you should be armed with information about the basic types of insurance, you'll most likely have to rely on your agent to explain the new ones and the various policies, so you need someone you can trust. Look for a person who will function as an ally, offering additional information and proposing alternatives, not forcing you to buy the product. If you get too much quick sell pressure, then contact someone else.

You will also need an agent who's familiar with the ways you can use insurance in your corporate life and not just some rookie agent who only knows about one or two of the uses for life insurance.

Knowing you need a trustworthy agent and actually finding one are two different things, as you may have guessed. One of the best ways to find a good agent is to ask for references from friends, family members, and co-workers. Also, if you belong to a local business group for a small businesses or entrepreneurs, this can be an excellent source for seeking a professional insurance adviser.

Insurance agents and brokers must obtain a license from the state in which they do business. Contact the state licensing agency and check to make sure the salesperson is licensed with no disciplinary proceedings pending. Many states provide this information online. You can also try calling the Better Business Bureau or state or local consumers affair agencies and ask about the number of consumer complaints filed against that salesperson, if any.

Finally, speak with several agents and note if the agent asks probing questions about your insurance needs or just tries to sell you a product. Also, compare the insurance products each agent offers to see which one is the best deal and best meets your needs.

One more thing before you sign on the dotted line, you should check the reliability of your insurance company. Such companies have, in the past, gone bankrupt. There is no national or federal insurance guaranty fund for Life Insurance Companies similar to FDIC insurance for bank depositors. In forty-seven states there is some sort of industry- sponsored state guarantee bond. As an example Colorado, Louisiana, New Jersey, and Washington, D.C., have no such funds. While these funds offer most policyholders the reasonable hope of not losing all their investments if the insurer goes broke, you certainly don't want to have to wait for state regulators to take charge of an insolvent company.

To avoid this scenario, check the reliability of the insurer from whom you plan to buy a policy. Several major companies rate the financial stability of insurance companies including AM Best, Moody's, Duff & Phelps, and Standard & Poor's. Inspect their websites for information. It's wise to check your insurance agency against one and even better two of these rating systems to be sure the company you're interested in gets top grade.

So much for the basics. let's look at some creative ways that you can use insurance products to keep the money that you have worked so hard to earn. One way to reduce your estate taxes is by transferring ownership of your life insurance policy. In this case, you can lower your beneficiary's estate tax burden by making sure you don't own your life insurance policy when you die. First things first, you don't need this unless your estate is likely to owe federal estate taxes at your death. As of right now, the estate tax affects only people who die leaving a taxable estate of more than a million dollars. Insurance is only included in an estate if the estate owns that policy. If the deceased person owns the policy, the full amount of the proceeds would be included in the federal taxable estate. If someone else owns the policy, the proceeds are not included.

Here's an example, Jane purchases and owns an insurance policy covering her life with a face value of $200,000 payable to her son, Jeff, as beneficiary. Jane's business partner, Bob, owns a second policy, also covering Jane's life for $400,000, payable to Bob. Bob will use these proceeds to pay Jeff, Jane's sole inheritor, the worth of Jane's interest in the business. If Jane dies, all the proceeds of Jane's policy, $200,000 are included in her federal taxable estate. However, none of the $400,000 from the policy Bob owns is part of Jane's federal taxable estate because Jane did not own the policy. It follows that if you want your life insurance proceeds to avoid federal estate tax, you may wish to transfer ownership of your life insurance policy to another person or entity.

Here are two ways you can do this: First, transfer ownership of your policy to any other adult, including the policy beneficiary. Second, you can create an irrevocable life insurance trust and transfer ownership to it. Be aware that some group policies, which many people participate in through work, don't allow you to transfer ownership at all. When transferring ownership of your policy to another person or persons, the first option involves a trade-off. Once the policy is transferred, you've lost all your power over it forever. You cannot cancel it or change the beneficiary.

To make this point bluntly, suppose you transfer ownership of your policy to your spouse and later get divorced. You cannot cancel the policy or recover it from your now ex-spouse. Nevertheless, in many situations, the trade-off is worth it, as, for example, when you transfer policy ownership to a child or children with whom you have a close and loving relationship.

You should also be aware of the tax treatment of this. The IRS has rules that determine who owns a life insurance policy when the insured person dies. Gifts of life insurance policies made within three years of death are disallowed for federal estate tax purposes and often for estate death tax purposes as well. This means that the full amount of the proceeds is included in your estate as if you have remained owner of the policy. Here's another example, Allen gives his $300,000 term life insurance policy to his business partner, Bob. Allen dies two years later. For federal estate tax purposes, the gift is disallowed and all the proceeds—$300,000—are included in Allen's taxable estate. If Allen had transferred the life insurance policy more than three years before his death, none of the proceeds would have been included in his taxable estate. The message here is obvious, if you want to give away a life insurance policy to reduce estate taxes, give the policy away as soon as possible. And then, don't die for at least three years!

Another IRS regulation provides that a deceased person who retained any incidence of ownership of a transferred life insurance policy is still considered the owner. The term "incidence of ownership" is simply legalese for keeping any significant power of the transferred insurance policy. Specifically, the proceeds of the policy will be included in your taxable estate if you have the legal right to do any of the following: change or name beneficiaries of the policy, borrow against the policy, pledge any cash reserve it has or cash it in, surrender, convert, or cancel the policy, or select a payment option (i.e., deciding if payments to the beneficiary is a lump sum or in installments).

When a life insurance policy is transferred from the original insured owner to a beneficiary, tax authorities regard the transaction as a gift. Under current gift tax rules, if you transfer a policy with a present value of more than $11,000 to another person, gift taxes will be assessed. However, keep in mind that the amount of gift tax paid will be far less than the amount of estate tax paid, if your policy had remained in your name and in your estate. This is because the proceeds payable under a policy when the insured dies are always considerably more than the worth of the policy while the insured lives.

Here's the example: Jim transfers ownership of his universal life insurance policy to his son, Owen. The value of the policy when he transfers it is $22,000. Under IRS rules, $11,000 of this is subject to gift tax. Jim dies four years after giving his son the insurance policy, which pays $300,000. The $300,000 is not included in Jim's federal taxable estate, neither are the proceeds considered income to Owen for federal income tax purposes.

So, if you're considering giving away an insurance policy, you'll want to know the present worth of that policy. If it's more than the amount of the annual gift tax exclusion, which is currently $11,000 or less, the IRS will assess a gift tax on the transaction. Under IRS rules, the value of a gift of a lifetime insurance policy for gift tax purposes is its cost—what it would cost to buy a similar policy, not the cash surrender value. You can find this value by asking your insurance agent. He or she will then give you the dollar value for gift tax purposes of your policy.

It is very easy to transfer ownership of a policy. You can give away ownership of your life insurance policy by signing a simple document called an "assignment" or a "transfer." To do this, notify the insurance company and use its assignment or transfer form. There's normally no charge to make the change. Also, you usually have to change the policy itself to specify that the insured is no longer the owner.

After the policy is transferred, the new owner should make any premium payments due. If the previous owner makes payments, the IRS might contend that the previous owner was keeping an incident of ownership and include the proceeds in the deceased owner's federally taxable estate, precisely what you are trying to avoid. If the new owner doesn't have sufficient funds to make the payments, you can give him or her money to be used for these payments.

If you give a paid-for single premium policy to a new owner, there's no question about who makes future payments. There aren't any Because it's paid for in full once it's purchased. Single premium life can be a particularly convenient type of policy to give to a new owner in order to reduce estate taxes; however, there can be a drawback here, too. If the value of the policy at the time of the gift exceeds the amount that is exempt from gift tax, $11,000 or less, the tax authorities will assess gift taxes on the excess amount.

By contrast, if the insured transfers ownership of a policy that has premiums due each year, and then every year gives the recipient a gift of less than $11,000 to pay for those premiums, no gift tax will be assessed.

The second way to transfer a life insurance policy is to create an irrevocable life insurance trust and then transfer ownership to that entity. An irrevocable trust is like a corporation, a legal entity distinct from any human being. Once you transfer ownership of life insurance to the trust, it owns the policy, not you, so the proceeds are not part of your estate.

Create a lifetime insurance trust rather than simply transferring a life insurance policy to someone else. One reason could be there's no one you want to give your policy to. In other words, you want the proceeds out of your taxable estate, but you want to exert legal control of the policy and avoid the risk of having an insurance policy on your life owned by someone else—perhaps a spouse or child you don't trust to pay policy premiums.

For example, the trust could specify that the policy must be kept in effect while you are alive, eliminating the risk that a new owner of the policy could decide to cash it in.

Here is a good example of a trust's use: Arlene is the divorced mother of two children in their twenties, who will be her beneficiaries. Neither is sensible with money. Arlene has an estate of $400,000 plus universal life insurance, which will pay $500,000 at her death. She wants to be sure her estate will not be liable for estate taxes and so desires to transfer ownership of her policy. However, there's no one Arlene trusts enough to give her policy to outright. With the controls, she can impose through a trust, however, she decides it's safe to allow her sister—the person she's closest to—to be the trustee of a life insurance trust for the policy. She creates a formal trust and transfers ownership of the life insurance policy to that trust.

After Arlene's death, her sister will handle the money for the children under the terms of the trust document. If you want to use such a life insurance trust, you must follow these points: The life insurance trust must be irrevocable. If you retain the right to revoke the trust, you'll be considered the owner of the policy and the proceeds will be subject to estate taxes. You cannot be the trustee. You must establish the trust at least three years before your death. If the trust has not existed for at least three years when you die, the trust is disregarded for estate tax purposes and the proceeds are included in your taxable estate.

So What?

Let's review what we've learned in this chapter. We have seen that it's really never too early to start thinking about and planning for your retirement. The need is real, as people are living longer and retiring earlier. And there are real doubts about whether or not Social Security will be there for you.

As a business owner, there are many strategies that are available to you that allow you to plan for your retirement. Using a combination of qualified tax deferred retirement plans as well as non-qualified plans can bring you a long way toward having what you need to fund your retirement. As well, look at some of the creative roles that life insurance can play in your retirement planning. In this case, it is worthwhile to spend some time seeking a qualified insurance specialist who is familiar with the retirement needs of an entrepreneur.

CHAPTER 11
Residual Income Retirement Planning

Mark 4:14-20 "*14 The sower soweth the word. 15 And these are they by the way side, where the word is sown; but when they have heard, Satan cometh immediately, and taketh away the word that was sown in their hearts. 16 And these are they likewise which are sown on stony ground; who, when they have heard the word, immediately receive it with gladness; 17 And have no root in themselves, and so endure but for a time: afterward, when affliction or persecution ariseth for the word's sake, immediately they are offended. 18 And these are they which are sown among thorns; such as hear the word, 19 And the cares of this world, and the deceitfulness of riches, and the lusts of other things entering in, choke the word, and it becometh unfruitful. 20 And these are they which are sown on good ground; such as hear the word, and receive it, and bring forth fruit, some thirtyfold, some sixty, and some an hundred.*"

One of the icons in the foodservice industry is Howard Schultz, the Chairman and CEO of Starbucks today. But I wonder how many of you know his real story.

Howard was born in the housing projects of Brooklyn, New York. But, unlike so many people who are born into that situation, Howard actually found his way out of the projects. And for him, his ticket was a full-ride football scholarship to the University of Northern Michigan. And that scholarship allowed him to do what he loved—play football. More importantly, it allowed him to get a college education. He became the first member of his family to actually graduate from college.

After college, Howard held several different jobs. They were mostly sales positions until he became the Sales Director for a Swedish housewares company called Hammarplast.

At Hammarplast, he sold Swedish drip coffeemakers to a small, one-store coffeehouse in Seattle called Starbucks. Now, Howard was intrigued by this. It was his best customer, so he decided to make the trip and meet the owner. He got on a plane and flew to Seattle. I don't know if this has ever happened to you before, but he fell in love from the moment he walked off the plane.

He loved Seattle. He had never been there before. He had actually never been west of the Mississippi. He loved the city, but when he walked into Starbucks, he just loved the environment they had created. As he sat down with the owners, he was amazed at the care they took in choosing and roasting the beans. When he left that day he thought, "I'm gonna be part of that company."

Well, it took Howard an entire year to convince the owners of Starbucks to employ him. They eventually did, and they brought him on as the Sales Director.

They sent him to Italy to work. And when he was there, he thought, "This is crazy!" On every corner, there was a coffeehouse—literally, every single corner. At first, he thought, "They can't drink this much coffee. Nobody can drink this much coffee."

But then he had an epiphany. He realized that the coffeehouses were more than that; they were a part of the "societal glue" of Italy. They were a place to meet a friend to have a relaxing afternoon or to just kick back and read a newspaper. They were a home away from home. They were a second office, if you will. You could meet and do business there. He came back with this idea from Italy and he said, "I've got it. We need to expand. We can take this one store, and we can grow it into thousands."

Well, the owners of Starbucks weren't interested. They said, "You know what, we're pretty happy with what we have here. We don't wanna grow. Thank you, but no thank you."

Howard made a choice that day. He said, "You know what? I see this so clearly that I'm gonna have to leave." He left and started his own coffeehouse called Giornali, which was so successful that the next year he came back and bought Starbucks for 3.8 million dollars. And the rest, as they say, is history, right?

Howard Schultz is recognized as one of the richest men in the world. He's taken that company of Starbucks and grown it to having coffeehouses in fifty-two countries around the world, with more than sixteen thousand locations.

The interesting thing about Starbucks, to me, is that it's one of those few companies personifying an industry. I mean, think about it. When you think about having a cup of coffee, what do you usually think about? You say, "We're gonna go get a Starbucks." I mean, I don't even drink coffee and I think of Starbucks.

I don't think it's just because they make the best cup of coffee. I think that it has a lot to do with the way that Howard runs the company. Starbucks is constantly praised for their friendly customer service. They're given award after award for the ambience they create within their stores. And Howard is constantly reminding his people of that one little phrase that has so much power in it. He's always saying, "We're not in the coffee business serving people, we're in the people business serving coffee." Now, I want you to think about that for just a minute. Howard Schultz is a great leader because he has his priorities straight. He understands what he is really in business for and who he actually reports to.

You see, all of us are in the people business, aren't we? Whether you're in management or you're a supervisor or the CEO, it doesn't matter—you're in the people business. We all interact with people every single day at work, at home, and at play.

In order to solve this cash flow problem, I would like to introduce you to a new way of looking at a business model that epitomizes the people business. It's new because of the explanation that I give for encouraging you to make it the foundation of your wealth-building plan. I call it the Residual Income Retirement Plan.

Do you need at least $3,000 per month in retirement income? Assuming a 5 percent withdrawal rate, you will need at least $720,000 in your investment account by age sixty-five. How much do you currently have? How much time do you have before your sixty-fifth birthday? How much do you currently earn? Can you invest enough each month to grow your account to $720,000? Most people can't, even if they saved 50 percent of their check.

The engine that drives the residual income retirement plan is network marketing. Conceptually, I want to teach you how to see the business model as a hybrid solution to your cash flow needs. In traditional security investing with a financial advisor or 401(k) plan, it is common for people to make an initial investment to fund their account and then to make monthly investments for mutual funds or stocks. Similarly, a person could make a one-time investment to become a distributor with a company and commit to making a monthly investment for the product or service. The home-based business provides the benefits of investing in a mutual fund, value stock, and income stock. Does that make sense?

When I think about the opportunity to generate an income as a network marketing professional, I think of value and income stocks. A value stock is a type of stock that is currently selling at a low price. Companies that have good earnings and growth potential but whose stock prices do not reflect this are considered value companies. Both the stock market and people investing in it are largely ignoring their stocks. Investors who buy value stocks—people who become distributors—believe that these stocks are only temporarily out of favor and will soon experience great growth. Any number of factors such as new management, a new product, or operations that are more efficient may make a value stock grow quickly.

Income stocks are stocks that pay higher-than-average dividends over a sustained period (e.g., residual income from building a sales team). These above-average dividends tend to be paid by large, established companies with stable earnings. Utilities and telephone company stocks are often classified as income stock types.

Income stocks are popular with those who are investing for steady income for a long time and who do not need much growth in their stocks' value, though some growth does occur. In this sense, investors who choose these stocks have something in common with bondholders—distributors who stay active for thirty-six months. Income stocks can actually be more profitable than bonds. To maximize income, some investors will even seek out companies that frequently raise dividends and are not saddled with debt (e.g., network marketers who are constantly seeking better timing or a compensation plan).

Like franchising, network marketing is not for everyone, but it has been lucrative and rewarding for many, and it is definitely worth investigating. By joining a network marketing company, becoming a network marketing professional, and operating it as a home-based business, you get ownership, you're in control of your return and generating sales, you get immediate tax benefits, you have an opportunity to replace your income, and you have an opportunity to create residual income for life.

Network marketing is a simple business in which you are paid commissions on products purchased by those who are in your distribution channel or network. If you choose to participate, you can build a worldwide distribution channel through which products are purchased. The tiered compensation structure is similar to almost every large sales organization in the world. Salespeople get commission, and sales managers get overrides or bonuses on top of that, and sales directors on top of that, and VPs on top of that. Like the standard franchise model, you have to pay and enter into an agreement in order to become a distributor. I assure you, the franchise fee of most traditional franchises dwarf the sign-up cost of any network marketing program by comparison.

Network marketing is a great opportunity for people to have their first business, their first sales role, and so on. I was first exposed to the industry in 1996, the week I graduated from West Point. It was my first exposure to personal growth and entrepreneurship, and that experience laid the foundation for the success I have had in every area of my life.

In order to achieve any degree of success, you must treat it as a business, and you must act as a professional. If you've never owned a business before, if you've never done sales before, and if you've never networked before, then you need to learn about these vital elements of the business. Find a mentor, not just from the network marketing industry but from established experts in leadership, success, sales, team building, and personal growth.

Network marketers who are serious about building a business should be reading and learning about business fundamentals, the latest sales and marketing techniques, strategies for networking and business development, and so on, not just swapping tips at their team's weekly or monthly meetings. Act like a network marketing professional, and people will treat you like one.

I believe network marketing is the very best business model developed so far for ordinary people to achieve extra-ordinary success. Network marketing has taken the concept of franchising and made some great improvements on it. Network marketing provides independent entrepreneurs with a ready-made, low-risk, proven, turnkey small business opportunity.

The following lists the six reasons why I recommend investing the time to explore network marketing opportunities:

1) **Low Capital Investment—Little or No Risk.** How much money do you need to become an independent network marketer? There is usually no fee required to start your networking business. You'll typically commit between a few hundred dollars to a few thousand dollars for your sales kit, training, sales and marketing materials, and your initial product inventory, if you even need it.

3) **Benefits and Tax Advantages of a Home-Based Business.** For most participants, network marketing is a home-based business, so you don't have the high overhead of a retail or office location. The equipment you need to begin your networking operation can be as simple as a telephone, desk, and file cabinet. And the potential tax advantages of owning and operating a legitimate home-based business represent one of the last forms of tax relief available to the average American today.

4) **No Employees—You are In Control.** As a network marketer, you are an independent contractor—the CEO of your own business. Think of it as "Me, Inc." You have no "employees." The men and women with whom you'll work are also CEOs, running their own independent networking businesses. In network marketing, you don't simply "own your own job"—you own your own business.

5) **More Choices—Part-Time, Full-Time, Travel, National, and Global Businesses.** Every network marketer is a volunteer—you don't "have" to do anything. You're free to work the days and hours you want, where you want, doing what you want. Perhaps most important of all, you're free to choose the people with whom you work.Although the majority of networkers work their businesses part-time—currently about 85 percent of the industry are part-time—more and more men and women are pursuing network marketing as a full-time career. Some work exclusively from their homes, some choose to set up formal offices, others enjoy traveling to other cities and even to other countries, building their businesses on a global scale.

6) **Personal and Professional Support.** In network marketing, you're in business for yourself, but not by yourself. Your network marketing corporation's success depends on your success. The corporation is your business partner, so it gives you the support possible, each step of the way. As a good franchise company

would do, a good network marketing company provides you with the product or service to market, plus a research and development department, new product development, field training, sales and marketing literature and promotional materials, a distributor service department, and more. Today every network marketing company is Internet friendly. You and your company are truly partners in a win-win opportunity.

Network marketing allows you to leverage your time, talent, and energy to earn commissions from the sales made by you and all the other people you sponsor in the business. My introduction to personal growth and entrepreneurship via network marketing was in 1996, the week I graduated from West Point. Although I have never created a six-figure income as a distributor, the knowledge and experience I gained laid the foundation for me to become a documented millionaire seven-years later at the age of thirty-two. Since that time, I have studied and participated in the industry and, more importantly, developed relationships with six- and seven-figure-per-year network marketing professionals representing several different products and services. I offer a generic seminar for those who are thinking about network marketing, and for those who are already in a network marketing business. This seminar is an opportunity to learn how to choose a good network marketing business, to enhance skills if you have a desire to become a network marketing professional, and to learn how to leverage network marketing to fund your retirement needs or desires. We discuss:

- How to distinguish a legitimate network marketing business from a pyramid or a scam
- How to find a good network marketing business
- How you know you are in the business and not just going to meetings
- How to prospect, invite, present, sponsor, teach, train, and coach
- How to create momentum
- How to create a long-term residual income.

If you succeed in generating income, it's going to be you who creates that success, not your boss or the market. And if you fail in generating income, it's going to be you who creates that failure, not your boss or the market. You're going to be the difference between success and failure! There will be people ready to guide you every step of the way, but they can't do it for you. They are there to work with you, but not for you.

CHAPTER 12
Planning Your Estate

Proverbs 13: 22 "*22 A good man leaveth an inheritance to his children's children: and the wealth of the sinner is laid up for the just.*"

In this chapter, I will discuss estate planning. While the phrase, estate planning, sounds like a topic just to be discussed at some time far in the future and then only if you're elderly, it's far more important than that. It's unfortunate that so many people shy away from even the thought of it because planning your estate is really about caring for your loved ones, seeing they are provided for, and making sure your hard-earned property is distributed according to your wishes. The general belief that you have to have a lot of money to do an estate plan or that you have to have a lot of assets is wrong. The truth of the matter is that if you have any concern at all at about being taken care of in your "golden years," and if you own property or any kind or assets, you should have an estate plan.

Your estate consists of all your property including your home and other real estate. Tangible personal property includes items such as cars and furniture. Intangible property includes items such as insurance, bank accounts, stocks and bonds, shares of your own corporation, pension, and Social Security benefits. An estate plan is your blueprint for where you want your property to go after you die. While a will is usually the most important part of an estate plan, it's not the only part. These days, it's common for a person to have a dozen wills—various ways of distributing property regardless of whether the person has a formal will. Pensions, life insurance, gifts, joint ownership, and trusts are but a few of the ways you can transfer property at or before death quickly and inexpensively. Estate planning is not just for the elderly. One glance at the news demonstrates that far too many young and middle-aged people die suddenly, often leaving behind minor children who need care and direction.

Estate planning needs to be factored into your overall financial plan along with tax planning and funding your retirement needs. If your financial or familial circumstances change later in life, it's usually easy and inexpensive to adjust your plan. It is important to understand that every state in this country has a plan for you, whether you plan your estate or not. It is called the law of intestacy. If you die intestate—without a will—your property still must be distributed. By not leaving a valid will or trust, or transferring your property in some other way such as through insurance, pension benefits, or joint ownership, you've left it up to Estate Law to write your will for you. This does not mean that your money will go to the state. That happens only in very rare cases where the person has no surviving relatives or even very remote ones. Dying intestate means that the state will make certain assumptions about where you'd like your money to go—assumptions with which you might not agree. Intestacy laws prefer blood over marriage assuming, perhaps wrongly, that the more closely related you are to someone, the more likely you'd want your property to go to that person. Some of your hard-earned money might end up with people who don't need it, for example, your grown child who already has more than you do. Meanwhile, others who might need the money more or who are more deserving could be short-changed such as that favorite niece of yours or your other child, who has had trouble finding steady work. Surviving relatives may squabble about who gets particular items of your property since you didn't make these decisions before you died.

Unfortunately, intestacy laws might also fail to provide adequate support for your spouse. For example, if you leave a spouse and no children, in many states, your spouse shares with your parents if they're alive. And your spouse may get as little as half of your property. Under the laws of one state, for instance, your spouse would get $5000 plus half the balance. Your parents will get the rest. In another state, your spouse would get $25,000 plus a half of the balance and your parents will get the rest. In several states, your spouse and parents would split 50–50. Most people want their spouse to get all their property but if they don't leave a will, that probably won't happen. The way to insure that your wishes are followed and that your other goals are achieved is to plan your estate. Only estate planning gives you the feeling of control that comes from knowing your family members are provided for as you wish. You decide who gets your property, when they get it, how they get it, and how much they get. Estate planning makes you the boss.

Your very first step toward an estate plan can be accomplished in an hour or even less. It requires nothing more than finding the documents that show you what you own and what you owe.

For starters, look for mutual funds statements, pension plan forms, and the title deed to any property you own. List any loans, mortgages, or lines of credit you have outstanding, as well as your credit cards. If people owe you money, note this as well. And if possible, try to find documents that show what you originally paid for stocks, bonds, and other securities in your portfolio. Here is a list to get you started. You may need to delete some categories or add others. Residents and other real estate; savings such as bank accounts, CDs, money markets; investments such as stocks, bonds, mutual funds, 401(k), IRA, pension, and other retirement accounts, life insurance policies and annuities, ownership interests in the business; and personal property such as motor vehicles, cars, boats, planes, jewelry. Yes, collecting these papers can be a bit of chore but simply having all the information at hand in a single folder makes it easy for an accountant or lawyer to figure out your financial situation. This could save you hundreds of dollars in professional fees. It also makes it easy for your heirs and yourself to see the extent of your estate at a glance.

Once you've estimated the value of your estate, you're ready to do some planning. Keep in mind that estate planning is not a one-time job. There are a number of changes that may call for a review of your plan. Take a fresh look at your estate plan if the value of your assets changes significantly; if you marry, divorce, or remarry; if you have a child; if you move to different state; if the executor of your will or the administrator of your trust dies or becomes incapacitated, or your relationship with that person changes significantly; if one of your heirs dies or has a permanent change in health; if the laws affecting your estate change.

Once you have papers together, it's time to ask yourself what you want to do with the wealth you will leave behind. At first, this may seem simple. Everything will go to your spouse or it will be divided equally among your children. But think about your possessions that might have particular meaning. You may want to consider making a special bequest of those items to specific individuals. Also, take note of any potential problem areas such as a family cottage that will have to be divided among several children, a business that has to be split, or how you're going to compensate your other children if you leave a favorite or valuable possession to one child.

Next, consider who you want to be the executor of your will. This person will be in charge of arranging your funeral, settling your final bills, filing your last tax return, and making sure that the provisions of your will are carried out as you wished. Obviously, it should be someone you trust such as your spouse, a child, a close friend, or a professional trustee. It helps if the person has some familiarity with legal or business matters. Ideally, too, your executor should live nearby and if you're getting on in years, it should be someone younger than yourself so he or she will be around when your family needs the person. You can name your husband or wife as executor but if so, you should also name an alternate executor in case you and your spouse die together.

By some estimates, fewer than half of adults in the United States have a will. This is shocking. If you die without a will, your property may languish in trust for months before your heirs can touch a penny of your money. Your wealth will ultimately be divided by the government according to a strict formula that apportions your possessions to your nearest relatives. Your wishes about who should get what, even if you have expressed those desires frequently in past conversations, won't matter.

In addition to a will, a lawyer can write up what's usually known as a continuing or enduring power of attorney. This is a relatively simple document but it's enormously powerful. It allows a person or people you choose to act on your behalf if you should become mentally incapacitated. Ideally, you should have two powers of attorney, one for your property and one for your personal care. You need one power of attorney for estate planning purposes. It is a continuing or enduring power of attorney for property. This remains in effect even if you become mentally incapacitated.

In contrast, an ordinary power of attorney is for property. For example, it gives someone the power to pay bills for you while you're on vacation. It is valid only as long as you are mentally competent. Therefore, it's not much use in estate planning. Your power of attorney for property can be as broad or as specific as you choose. But in most cases, it allows your chosen administrator access to your bank accounts if you become unable to function. This can be very useful for your family. It means that if you're hovering in a coma, the mortgage and other bills will still get paid.

The power of attorney for your personal care can be even more important. It allows your chosen administrator to make decisions about the care that you will receive if you're too sick or confused to make decisions for yourself. This can stand everything from deciding on pain management and heroic resuscitation measures to selecting your nursing home.

The next step toward creating a sound estate plan is to understand how estates are taxed. Federal gift and estate tax law permits each taxpayer to transfer a certain amount of assets free from tax during his or her lifetime or at death. In addition, certain gifts valued at $10,000 or less can be made that are not counted against this amount. The amount of money that can be shielded from federal gift tax is determined by the Federal Unified Tax Credit. The credit is used during your lifetime when you make certain taxable gifts and the balance, if any, can be used by your estate after your death. There are a number of estate planning methods that can be used to minimize federal taxes on your estate.

The first one that many people don't think about is giving away assets during your lifetime. Federal tax law generally allows each individual to give up to $10,000 per year to anyone without paying gift taxes subject to certain restrictions. That means you can transfer some of your wealth to your children or others during your lifetime to reduce your taxable estate. For example, you could give $10,000 a year to each of your children and your spouse could do likewise for a total of $20,000 per year to each child. You may make $10,000 annual gifts to as many people as you wish. You may also give your child or another person more than $10,000 a year without having to pay federal gift taxes, but the excess amount will count against the amounted shielded from tax by your unified credit. For example, if you gave your favorite niece $30,000 a year for the last three years, you would have reduced your unified credit by $60,000—a $20,000 excess gift each year.

Other estate planning measures involve the use of trusts. Trusts have been used for hundreds of years for tax savings and estate planning. But few people realize the enormous potential for using trusts for tax planning as well for privacy for you and your estate.

The idea behind the trust is very straightforward. A trust is a private, contractual arrangement between several parties for holding, managing, and investing assets. The parties to the trust are the grantor, the person creating the trust, also known as the settlor or trustor; and the trustee, the person or entity holding title to the assets and the beneficiaries, for whose benefit the trust is established. A trust created for one's benefit is called a self-settled trust. It is one in which the creator and beneficiary are the same person. A trust created during the life of the grantor is called an inter vivos or living trust. An inter vivos trust can be revocable (taken back) or modified by the grantor, or irrevocable, which means once created, it cannot be revoked.

Why should you use a trust for estate planning purposes? The typical living trust is created by an individual for his or her own benefit. He or she also names himself or herself as trustee.

An example is the "John Smith family living trust." Upon John's death, a successor trustee is named to hold and manage the trust property. This is typically his spouse, sibling, or a bank trust department. Although John is the beneficiary during his life, the trust will name his family as alternate beneficiary upon his death.

One of the main reasons why living trusts are used is to avoid probate. Upon your death, the assets remaining in your estate are distributed according to the instructions of a will. If there is no will, it is distributed according to the rules set forth by state law. The probate court is involved throughout the process, adding time, cost, and aggravation. The will is now public record for everybody to see. If most of your assets are owned in trust, these assets are neither subject to probate nor are they on display for anyone who wants to see them. The trustee, according to the instructions of the trust agreement, either distributes the assets outright to your heirs, the alternate beneficiaries, or holds them in trust until they reach a certain age. Your trust can hold assets such as real estate in multiple states without the need for probate in any of these states. A trust, unlike a corporation, is not registered with the state.

There are no public records of officers, directors, and shareholders. There are no minutes of directors and shareholders' meetings. The trustee keeps control of the trust records and the identity of the beneficiaries in his or her files. A trustee will not reveal this information without a court order.

Revocable living trusts are called tax neutral—there are no tax consequences of transferring property into trust. According to Sections 671 to 678 of the Internal Revenue Code, the property is treated as still being owned by the grantor. The logic is that since the grantor can revoke the trust, it still belongs to him or her for tax purposes.

For example, if you owned rental property and recorded on schedule E of your federal income tax return, a transfer into a revocable living trust for which you are the beneficiary, it would not change your recording. Compare this to transferring property into a corporation, which is a separate taxpayer, even if you own all of the stock of the corporation.

To determine if a living trust is right for you and your estate, first think about the advantages. There are a growing number of ways to transfer assets to inheritors free of probate within weeks or at most, months of death. These include making gifts before death, adding a pay-on-death designation to a bank account, or holding your house in joint tenancy with right of survivorship with your spouse or partner and naming a beneficiary for life insurance and retirement accounts. Only the living trust can be used for all types of property and offers the broad planning flexibility of a will. With the living trust, for example, you can name alternate beneficiaries to inherit property if your primary beneficiary dies before you do. This is something you cannot accomplish with joint tenancy or a pay-on-death bank account. A living trust provides some privacy issues and an ability to escape probate. It will not become part of the public record unless a trustee or a beneficiary demands court approval of accounts. Probate records are always open to the public. Does everyone need a living trust? Living trusts do have a downside.

Compared to wills, living trusts are considerably more time consuming to establish, they involve more ongoing maintenance and are more trouble to modify. And if you hire a lawyer, and you should, you'll probably pay upward of $1,000 for the document. These drawbacks are clearly outweighed by the benefits for people who have large estates and therefore will achieve big savings by avoiding probate. The same goes for older people who are likely to die sooner. Living trusts make a lot of sense for most middle-income people in decent health who are under age fifty-five or sixty. Remember, a living trust does nothing for you during your life. It follows then that there is usually little reason for a forty-year-old to worry about probate cost for many years. In the meantime, a serviceable will, which is easier to establish and live with, will do a fine job at transferring your property to your loved ones in the unlikely event that you die without warning.

Another reason why it makes very little sense for a healthy younger person of moderate means to worry about probate avoidance is that the problem may go away. In just the last ten years, easy-to-use probate avoidance techniques, such as being able to name the beneficiary to inherit securities free of probate, have gained wide acceptance. It's a good guess that this trend will accelerate.

After the aspect of age, the biggest factor in deciding whether or not to create a living trust is wealth. At the risk of oversimplifying, the wealthier you are, the more you can save for your inheritors by avoiding probate. For example, a forty-five-year-old with $10,000,000 might conclude it's not too soon to think about probate avoidance, just in case. A forty-five-year-old with $300,000 might sensibly decide fifteen years or more.

The kinds of assets you own are significant as well. Owning a small business, or assets you don't want tied up during probate, might encourage you to create a living trust at a younger age. Even if there's only a small chance that you'll die soon, you don't want to risk making your executor report to a judge for a year or more. Finally, if you're married and you and your spouse plan to leave the bulk of your property to one another, there is less reason to think about living trusts at an early age. If, like many couples, you own your big assets together in joint tenancy, or if available in your estate as survivorship community property, probate will not be necessary for those assets. And for other property, most states let surviving spouses use expedited probate procedures that are faster and cheaper than standard probate.

Now that we have reviewed the basics about trusts and discussed the role of living trusts, let's look at some more advanced ways of using trusts for estate planning purposes.

Federal tax law generally permits you to transfer assets to your spouse without incurring gift or estate taxes, regardless of the amount. This is not however, without its drawbacks. Marital deductions may increase the total combined federal estate tax liability of the spouses upon the subsequent death of the surviving spouse. To avoid this problem, many couples choose to establish a bypass trust. Bypass trusts or credit shelter trusts can give a couple the advantages of the marital deduction while utilizing the unified credit to its fullest.

Let's say, for example, that a married couple has a federal taxable estate worth $2,000,000 or $1,000,000 each. Using the marital deduction, if the wife dies in 2013, the full $1,000,000 can be left to the husband without incurring taxes. However, if the husband dies in 2014, and passes his $2,000,000 estate onto the children, taxes will be levied on the excess over the amount of assets shielded by the unified credit. The equation is: $2,000,000 minus $1,000,000 equals $1,000,000, subject to estate tax. With the bypass of a credit shelter trust, the first spouse to die can leave the amount shielded by the unified credit to the trust. The trust can provide income to the surviving spouse for life. Then, upon the death of the surviving spouse, the assets are distributed to beneficiaries such as children. This permits the spouse who dies first to fully utilize his or her unified credit. If the trust document is drawn properly, the assets in the trust are not included in the surviving spouse's estate. Thus, the surviving spouse's estate will be smaller and can also utilize the unified credit. In that example, the surviving spouse's estates would not have to pay federal estate taxes. Because both partners have made use of their unified credits, the couple is able to pass on a substantial estate, tax-free to their beneficiaries.

Life insurance trusts can be designed to keep the proceeds of a life insurance policy out of your estate and give your estate the liquidity it needs. Generally, you could fund the life insurance trust either by transferring an existing life insurance policy or by having the trust purchase a new policy. To avoid inclusion in your estate, such trust must be irrevocable, meaning that you cannot dissolve the trust or change the terms of the trust if you change your mind later. With proper planning, the proceeds from life insurance held by the trust may pass to trust beneficiaries without income or estate taxes. This gives them cash, which may be used to help pay estate taxes or other expenses such as death or funeral costs.

Yet another technique is what is known as an AB Trust or a QTIP trust. Each person is entitled to have the first $2,045,085 of his or her estate passed to his or her heirs without estate taxes. This is referred to as the unified credit.

An AB Trust is a trust designed to make sure the unified credit of each spouse is used to the full extent possible while allowing the surviving spouse to have the use of the assets of the deceased spouse during the remainder of the surviving spouse's lifetime.

A QTIP trust permits a spouse to transfer assets to his or her trust while still maintaining control of the ultimate disposition of those assets at the spouse's death. QTIP trusts are particularly popular in situations where a person is married for a second time and who has children from a first marriage for whom he or she wants to reserve assets.

Another way of using trusts that you should keep in mind is something called an "irrevocable life insurance trust." It works quite simply by transferring small amounts of the estate equal to the amount of a life insurance premium to an irrevocable life insurance trust. A person can reduce the size of his or her taxable estate while creating a much larger asset—the life insurance proceeds outside of the estate. The life insurance proceeds are generally not taxable to the recipient.

Another strategy to consider is forming a family limited partnership. The family limited partnership provides a valuable estate planning tool to assist families in transferring ownership of family owned closely held businesses to the next generation and in protecting family assets from creditors. It also permits taxation of partnership income at the children's lower tax rates. Another attractive feature of the family limited partnership is its flexibility and revocability.

Yet another tool is called the "private annuity plan." A private annuity is a sale of an asset to a younger generation in exchange for an unsecured promise to pay annual amounts to the seller for the seller's lifetime. The sold asset is thus removed from the seller's estate, although the amounts of the payments to the seller, unless spent, will be part of the seller's estate.

As part of the estate planning of your business, you should also think about making use of a qualified Family Owned Business Interest (QFOBI). The Internal Revenue Code permits a qualified Family Owned Business Interest to be deducted from a gross estate. To qualify for the deduction, the following requirements must be met:

1. The descendants or family members must have owned and participated in the business for at least five of the last eight years.
2. The business interest must make up at least 50 percent of the descendant's adjusted gross estate. The descendant and his or her family must have owned 50 percent of the business.
3. The descendant must have been a U.S. citizen or resident.
4. And finally, the business must be located in the United States.

If you and your business can meet these criteria, look at the advantages of a QFOBI.

Here are two more estate planning hints: If you hold a significant amount of real estate in your estate, look at the special valuations that may be available to you. For federal estate tax purposes, Real Estate is usually valued at its highest and best use value. This can sometimes produce unfair results such as where a family farm is located (e.g., adjacent to more valuable commercial Real Estate). To address this unfairness, the Internal Revenue Code permits certain Real Estate to be valued at its actual use rather than its highest and best use. Specific requirements must be met, so make sure that your adviser is up to speed on this.

Finally, if you're going to be making donations to a charity, take a look at your charitable transfer options. Lifetime charitable transfers or gifts to charities upon death can reduce the size of the estate and therefore reduce estate taxes. Lifetime gifts provide the added benefit of an income tax deduction. Gifts can also be made in a manner that lets the donor retain the right to use the gifted asset or income there until death.

Before we leave this section on estate planning and the use of trusts, let's look at how your corporation can be used for estate planning purposes. Corporations, all on their own, can offer many advantages for estate planning purposes. In this case, you would form a corporation and then issue stock in the corporation to your heirs, divided any way you wish according to likes, dislikes, or earned advantages. The stock should be issued as non-voting until your death or the death of, say, both parents. You place within the private corporation all your assets—house, autos, stocks—all personal assets of value or importance. Then, when you die, the stock voting rights of the stockholders you have preselected become activated. In this way, they can take control of the business.

To do this, you have to have carefully written instructions in the bylaws of your corporation. There is no probate. There are no holds on bank accounts. The corporation continues to function as if you had only replaced the chairman of the board. If there are any personal debts of partners, they should be evaluated and placed into their proper categories and charged against the individual accounts in order to preserve the basic status of the corporation itself. There should be no quarrel, just good business attended and that without dispute. At the death of a partner, the remaining partners must bring the records up to date. Settle the intended instructions to cover properly all past decisions, and restructure the corporate officers' roster to suit the needs for the convenience of ongoing business and settlement. In this way, you set up the family estate as a corporation that simply carries on after your death, as established or desired according to your wishes, after your resignation through retirement or death, or whatever you might choose as the criteria.

Now consider the powerful ways that you can use the basic protection of a corporation, combined with the power of a limited partnership. You can form a business corporation with no assets and no liabilities. Its stock is worthless at this point. Next, you can effect the sale of this stock from the corporation to your investors' heirs at 1 percent share or some other very low rate. Distributed by the pro-rated amount you choose, giving each share the percentage of the firm that you wish—10 percent, 25 percent, or whatever you want it to be. Since the stock is being sold to your eventual heir, it's not a gift.

One object of a stock is to increase its value over a period of time. If the stock does increase in value, then there's nothing out of the ordinary. The next step is to form a limited partnership appointing you as general partner and your heirs as limited partners. The sole purpose of this limited partnership is to hold and control by means of irrevocable proxies, the stock of the corporation you just formed. Remember that in a limited partnership, the general partner manages the business and the limited partners have nothing to do with running it. Also bear in mind that the business of this limited partnership is to hold the stock of the new corporation. This means the general partner—you—will vote the stock at any stockholders' meeting. All of the stockholders—you and your investors' heirs—put their newly acquired stock into the limited partnership. In return, you could then become general partner and a 2 percent limited partner. For example it could be 1 percent for you and 1 percent for your spouse. Your investors' heirs become 98 percent limited partners. The general partner—you—will manage the business. You vote the stock.

This limited partnership will have a set life in existence for a certain number of years. How many years? Well that number depends on you. Make the term long enough so that when the limited partnership ends, you either won't be around or won't want to control the corporation any longer.

One of the important features of any limited partnership is that it can be drawn up so that it ends upon the death of any of the general partners. When you die, the limited partnership terminates and the other partners—your heirs—take their 98 percent of the stock in the corporation and continue as they always have. Only your 2 percent of the stock will go through probate and hopefully your estate will be small enough because of your wise prior planning to eliminate any problems. This is a very useful way of transferring a business to your heirs.

Assuming you perform the steps that we just discussed, your heirs will now have the stock and own the company. But you, by virtue of your general partnership, have complete control of the corporation. While you're alive, you control the company's assets, its money, and Real Estate—everything the corporation owns. You can also sell these assets and pay yourself the money or unto the assets, pay for any and all reasonable expenses, travels, medical expenses, and so forth. You can basically do anything you want for as long as you live.

In any estate planning system using a corporation, a key component is placing your assets and money into the corporation. You can do this any number of ways, depending on your particular situation.

For example, you could sell the assets to the corporation in exchange for a Demand Promissory Note to mature in fifty years, or whatever term you deem appropriate. Take money out of the corporation anytime you wish and mark it as "Due against this promissory note." The wording of the note should state that in the event of your death, any amount remaining payable to you by the corporation under the note is automatically forgiven. The Demand Promissory Note should bear interest in the range of 6 to 8 percent and state that the corporation pays you the interest when it becomes due. Where does the corporation get money for this? From you.

You're simply transferring the money from yourself to the company. Also, you might consider the possibility of taking a contract from your corporation in exchange for your services rendered. This means that your company provides the lifetime contract and guarantee that the corporation will provide for you, in exchange for the services that you provide to the company. This can include all of your medical bills, convalescent care, and other such expenses. This is similar to purchasing a lifetime annuity whereby a lump sum of money is converted into an income string.

Be careful of possible tax consequences here. Make sure you know your tax regulations and check them with a competent tax adviser. Remember, when you put your assets into the corporation, the value of its stock increases but there are no taxes until such time as dividends are paid by the corporation or the stock is sold. In both cases, this matter is one over which you have complete control and for which you can adequately plan in advance to legally avoid taxes and best plan your estate.

A word of note about placing Real Estate into a corporate structure or trust: If you place your personal residence into such a structure, you will lose your mortgage interest deductibility or in the case of commercial property, the depreciation tax deduction. So if your estate is small and the Real Estate is a long way from being fully owned with many years of mortgage payments remaining, it's probably not advantageous to include it in this long-term planning, for now. On the other hand, if the estate is larger and the Real Estate is owned outright or has few mortgage payments left, the advantages to this approach can be significant. If more than one property is involved, you might want to consider a separate corporation for each property. The nice part about holding property in the corporation is that when it comes time to sell, you have the option of selling the corporation, which won't trigger transfer taxes.

The bottom line of all the strategies we've discussed is this: When you die, your heirs should already own all that you want them to have. Since your heirs already own your estate when you pass on, there's no transfer, no probate, no big taxes, and no problems. With this estate planning, you know what is going to happen to your loved ones when you die. Everything you have worked for and acquired is going to the one(s) you leave it to. There won't be a long, drawn out probate case in court and that should give you peace of mind. You don't have to worry about little or nothing existing for your heirs once all the legal fees, expenses, inheritance taxes, and so forth are paid. What can take years through legal delay, astronomical expenses, waste, and agony for the ones you love is accomplished by them at their stockholders' meeting through the election of directors and officers. The transition is fast and problem-free. Everything continues without interruption. You have the peace, joy, satisfaction, and confidence in knowing that your loved ones have exactly what you intend for them to have.

Individual circumstances demand individual planning with careful understanding, if possible, prior to the need or execution of any estate planning program. If there is a complicated array of things to consider, these need to be sorted out with knowledgeable personnel.

Have the next in line be aware of what is expected of him or her. Remember, corporations never die. They just get a new president. Take advantage of this corporate immortality. Put what you have into a corporation and the corporation will live past you to successfully distribute your assets to the people you wish to have them. This eliminates the normal pitfalls of estate planning, probate, and taxes.

In summary, spend a little time today thinking about planning your estate. Don't delay. Sure, there's paperwork and planning involved but approach this no differently than you do when you undertake maintaining new corporate records and documentation. You have to take some time to plan for your future and you've got to make sure that it's done in an orderly fashion. Don't leave that confusion to someone else. By taking the time now, you ensure your estate passes to whom you want, when you want, with a minimum amount of taxes, probate, and paperwork.

CHAPTER 13
Life is Rich

Hebrews 11:1-3 *"11 Now faith is the substance of things hoped for, the evidence of things not seen. 2 For by it the elders obtained a good report. 3 Through faith we understand that the worlds were framed by the word of God, so that things which are seen were not made of things which do appear."*

In this book, I have shared with you in detail the financial danger and what you need to know about the financial opportunities in becoming an entrepreneur. The first chapters took you through the process of creating, planning, and then growing your business. Next, I shared some of the many sources available to find your business as well as the best way to structure your affairs. We explored the different business entities that are available from corporations to limited liability companies. These entities can protect your assets, legally reduce your taxes, and keep your financial affairs private. Finally, I showed you how corporations and trusts can be used to fund your retirement needs and how they can be used effectively for estate planning purposes to let you make money, keep money, and pass your assets along to your heirs. So now what?

Do you feel that you have the potential and the capacity to accomplish more than you have so far? Do you know that there are things in your life that are holding you back? Does fear sometimes reach you and grab you by the throat and prevent you from dreaming your dreams or attempting to fulfill your goals?

If so, then I want to talk to you for a few minutes about my mentoring program, which is designed to help you identify your passion and design the lifestyle you desire so that you can live your passion full-time.

You see, I believe that each one of us has a purpose and a reason to be on this planet. I believe we are capable of much more than what we have accomplished thus far in our lives. I don't know anyone who hasn't just "settled" in their life. No one has the money of Bill Gates and the body of Will Smith or Halle Berry, the relationships of Oprah Winfrey, and the faith of Joel Osteen. No one has all these things in his or her life. We've all settled and the result is we're not creating our dreams. We're not living up to our potential. Most people are not flourishing—they're languishing, hoping for a decent ending.

Hebrews 11:1 reads "Now faith is the substance of things hoped for, the evidence of things not seen." The reality is this: hope is not a strategy. The other reality is that your best thinking got you to where you are today. In other words, you have created your current situation and if you created it then you can change it.

Too many people believe that practice makes perfect. Nothing could be further from the truth. Practice makes permanent. Practice is what creates our habits and our habits are what are running the bulk of our lives and thus creating our future. See, I believe that each of us is in charge of our own destiny and each of us was born to be great. I did not say that each of us are born great, but rather born to be great. Daily habits done daily build the character required to focus on perfect practice, which leads to perfect.

Unfortunately, part of being human is to see if we can do the least amount and somehow get the most. We live in a culture that seems to be based on instant gratification, which is a surefire formula for failure in every aspect of your life.

The problem is that none of us can see ourselves swing. We are all too often unconscious of what we're doing to sabotage our lives. I believe, the higher you want to go and the more success you desire in any endeavor, the greater the likelihood is that you will need a mentor or a personal coach.

A sniper is a highly trained soldier who specializes in shooting targets with modified rifles from incredibly long distances. They're also adept in stealth, camouflage, infiltration, and observation techniques. A sniper team consists of a sniper and a spotter. The two-man team offers many advantages over the lone sniper in the field. The spotter carries a special scope that is much more powerful than the scope on a sniper rifle. The spotter uses the scope to help the sniper observe objectives and set up the shot. The two soldiers work together to get to the objective safely and discreetly and then set up a position. Here's the general process:

- The sniper team uses maps or photographs to determine the best route to the objective.
- Team members walk or "stalk" (more on this later) from the drop-off point to the objective.
- They set up a position.
- They verify that the position is well camouflaged.
- They establish an escape route and a second, well-camouflaged fallback position in the event they are separated.
- They locate the target or know it's on its way.
- They get into position.
- The sniper takes a spot on the ground that offers the best field of fire.

- The spotter lies on the ground next to and slightly behind the sniper. The spotter places the spotter scope so that it is as close to looking down the rifle barrel as possible.
- They work together to range the target, read the wind, and angle and adjust for other variables that may affect the shot.
- They wait for the target.
- Take the shot and get out of the area.

Look at any professional athlete, and standing beside him or her is a coach who can watch the athlete perform. Even Tiger Woods, often considered the greatest golfer in the world, has a full-time coach for only one reason—he can't see himself swing. He can't see what needs to be corrected when something goes wrong. Furthermore, he doesn't know what to do to make himself better. His coach is there to watch his form as he swings and to help correct and guide him to his full potential in the fastest amount of time and to help him achieve the excellence he desires. There's no trial and error and no guessing on what to do differently. The coach sees the problem and corrects it.

I want you to think about that last statement and think about who in your life is watching you "swing." Who is your coach or your mentor? More importantly, is the person qualified to guide you where you want to go? Has the person "been there and done that"? My experience is that most people don't have someone to guide them and who will tell them the truth.

The reason is because telling the truth can be risky—people tend to get their feelings hurt. Everyone is busy protecting the relationship, and the reality is that the relationship is often superficial or fake to begin with; my mask being in relationship with your mask. It just doesn't work very well. The problem with this scenario is this: you can't change a lie. You can't change what you aren't aware of or conscious of, and most of us are unaware of what we're doing or thinking that is producing the results in our lives.

Following one of my events in 2013, I sent out a research survey to my list and posted it to Facebook. I wanted to find out what people really wanted so that I could give them that.

Everyone has been to a seminar in which you get all wound up for a week or two after the event and then slowly backslide into your old habits and ways of doing things. So, these students wanted a seminar in which they learned some skills and then went out and practiced for a few months. They then wanted to get back together again with the same group of people to review how each participant did and to learn some more skills.

They said that one of their biggest problems was finding a group of likeminded people to associate with and to learn with. It seems it is very hard to find other entrepreneurs who are dedicated to building something meaningful in their lives and who are going for it full steam ahead. They said they needed a team of people who could support them and encourage them in between meetings. They wanted someone they could report their progress as well as their mistakes and slips to who would actually care about them and want them to succeed.

They said they wanted to deal in absolute confidence and trust so that they could be absolutely honest about their issues and problems and ideas without being concerned about anything that was said leaving the room or being disclosed to someone who is not part of the group.

They said they wanted to have access to me in between meetings so that if they got stuck, they could contact me and get my advice and help. They said they not only needed the business tools to be successful, they needed some motivation and tools to help them with balance and clarity and to be successful in their lives.

I was listening very intently while they were telling me what they wanted and what it needed to look like. Fortunately, I had my recorder. I looked at this group of people when they had finished telling me what they wanted and I asked this question: "If this is what you want and I create it and give it to you, will this be of value to you? Will you enroll in this program?" And they said yes.

That was the birth of my mentoring program. The topics we cover in each mentoring group are different because the issues and problems faced by the students are different. Some of the topics we will have covered in previous groups include: debt management, raising money, getting started, figuring out in which direction to go, communications, sales, marketing, negotiations, building the team, expansion, focus, balance, time management, leadership, clarity, creating financial freedom, finding new opportunities, producing passive income, turning ideas into reality, Real Estate strategies and investing, and forming networks and strategic alliances.

Each group lists up to fifty different issues and problems they want to discuss, and that is just in the first weekend. And we cover every single item on the list. I continuously incorporate the ideas and issues that go into my mentoring program—every single item. My mentoring groups are limited to thirty people. The course consists of two three-day weekends. The meetings are about four months apart. I'm the only teacher at my events. I work one-on-one with each individual student on his or her specific issues and problems.

Every student has a specific list of goals to work on and teams to work with between meetings. Every student has a specific team of people to help, encourage, and critique him or her. These groups become so close that many of them will decide to keep in touch and hold reunions months after the mentoring program has been completed. The bonds that are possible really are that close.

If you want to see where you'll be in five years, look at the books you read and the people you associate with. This issue of team is crucial. People's lives are a direct reflection of the expectations of their peer group. You will adapt to gain or keep the approval of your peer group. Whomever you spend time with is the person you tend to emulate, so take a hard look at who's on your team and who's in your peer group. Do the people around you have higher standards and don't let you get comfortable? We all know that to get better at anything requires us to be with people who can outperform us.

My only requirement for attending this program is that you have desire. I don't care how old, young, rich, poor, or educated you are. Without desire, nothing can change. Without a desire to create spectacular excellence in your life I can't help you, and no one else can either. I can't care more about your dreams than you do. People who know they have settled and are in a rut—people who feel they're not living up to their potential, people who want to be inspired to create their destiny, people who want to create financial freedom in their lives, people who want excellence—are the types of people who attend my mentoring program.

People who are happy with the status quo who feel average is acceptable, who can hardly wait for the workday to end so that they can race home, prop their feet up, open a can of beer, and watch television for the rest of the evening are not the kind of people I can work with. People who are content to tiptoe through life only to arrive at their door safely are all people who should definitely not attend this program.

The difference between these two different groups of people is that desire to change and grow and be inspired to create their destiny. My thought is this: Success does not go on sale. There is no layaway plan for success. Success requires full payment upfront. Success is predictable and so is failure. Unsuccessful people tend to look for pleasing methods. Successful people focus on pleasing results.

Too many people say they are unwilling to pay the price for creating financial freedom or spectacular relationships or great health. That's backward thinking. You don't pay the price for any of these, you reap the rewards. When you stop to think about it, you pay the price for *not* creating financial freedom, for *not* creating wonderful relationships or fantastic health. All too often, however, we try to change our lives by trying to change our outcomes or circumstances.

Have you ever made a New Year's resolution? Most of us have. Have you ever made a New Year's resolution and not kept it? Most of us have had that experience as well. Why is that? Why do we commit to change things in our lives only to gradually backslide and then totally forget about it? I believe that a commitment we make to ourselves should be no less sacred than a commitment we make to others.

I think the main reason we make New Year's resolutions and then don't keep them is because we're focused on changing the outcome or the circumstance instead of the thoughts that produce the desired result in our lives. In other words, I think our results are nothing more than a logical consequence of our habits, which are a result of our actions, which are a result of our choices, which are a result of our thoughts. In other words, our thoughts have created our circumstances or given them meaning. And it is our thoughts that need to be redirected and changed if we are to be successful in changing our lives. The law of cause and effect is alive and well. Our thoughts and our choices are the cause. Our habits and our outcomes are the effects.

> *Thoughts lead to Feelings*
> *that lead to Actions*
> *that lead to Results.*

People who are fixated on changing their outcomes are usually people who are laying blame or justifying why they have those problems or circumstances. In reality, these people are victims and have a victim's mentality. Victims are never responsible for their lives. It's always someone else's fault. The problem here is that we can't fix what we can't see and we can't change something we didn't create. In other words, if we don't take responsibility for our outcomes, we will never attempt to change them because we had no part in creating them in the first place.

The first thing people must do is to become aware of what they are doing or not doing to create the results in their lives. The price of awareness is responsibility. If you are aware, then you will be responsible, and if you are responsible, then you acknowledge that you created it, and what you have created you can change. My thought is this: change your mind, change your life.

A study was completed of the graduates of the Harvard Business School. What they found is that 3 percent of the Harvard MBAs are making 97 percent of the money. On average, the 3 percent was earning ten times more than the other 97 percent put together. How can that be? These are all very, very smart people. They have had the exact same classes from the exact same instructors for the exact same length of time. They all read the exact same books. How can 3 percent be making 97 percent of the money? I know the answer to that question and I will give you the tools to create the same results in your life.

The mentoring program is about flourishing, not just getting by. It's about facilitating your dreams and developing your potential. It's about providing you with a compass, inspiring your being. It's about motivating you and holding you accountable for your actions. As Abraham Maslow has said, self-actualization is when you must be what you can be. I believe that being anything less than excellent and spectacular is a waste of time. Aristotle said we are what we do repeatedly; excellence, therefore, is not an act it's a habit.

Your best thinking got you to where you are today with your life. If you could have done it differently, you would have, but you didn't so you couldn't. Think about that. If your best thinking got you to where you are right now, would it be helpful for you to have some different thoughts, to have someone watch you "swing" and to correct your swing so that you can produce better results in your life? Are there some areas of your life that you know you need to change, but you just haven't done it? See, change is easy. You don't have to do anything, just sit back and change will happen.

Change is automatic, growth is not. Do you have a growth plan for your life? Growth is not an automatic process. You must have a plan. Where you are in your life today is a direct of reflection of your standards. The quality of your life is nothing more than the quality of your standards. I believe that to change your life, you must change your standards, and that requires change and growth and a plan. If you have the desire to take your life and your business to the next level, if you want to create spectacular results in every aspect of your life, if you want to live your passion full-time, then my mentoring program is for you. As Mahatma Gandhi said, "Let us become the change we seek in this world."

Thank you for your time, thank you for your commitment to yourself, and thank you for your interest in my program.

Be Blessed.

WHAT I LEARNED OF VALUE

If I tell you, you forget. If I teach you, you remember.
If I involve you, you will learn.

ORGANIZATIONAL COACHING & TRAINING:
We work with teams and organizations to provide customized training and coaching to develop leaders.

The coaching services provided to the client include a powerful, comprehensive process for personal development and transformation, as designed jointly with the client. Coaching may address specific personal projects, work successes or general conditions in the client's life as they choose.

STEP 1: ASK THE RIGHT QUESTIONS (80% is Psychology)

- **What Results Are You Committed To Creating In Your Life And Business?**
  Where is your ultimate target? What are you committed to achieving? What kind of lifestyle and identity are you committed to creating? What will be the primary question that you will ask yourself each day? What are the beliefs that will empower you to create these results?

- **What does your life and business look like today?**
  What results have you been producing financially in the past? How have you felt about finances, money, or lack of wealth? What have been the beliefs that have held you back? Are you struggling? Are you fearful of the future? Where were you financially?

STEP 2: FIND THE RIGHT ANSWERS (20% is Mechanics)

- **What specific actions will you decide to take to begin to close the gap between where you are and where you're committed to being now?**
  What are you going to master? What new skills and knowledge are you going to learn? What belief are you going to adopt? What are you going to get rid of that no longer adds value to your life? What coaching are you going to get?

"Success will never be a big step in the future, success is a small step taken just now."

~ *Jonatan Martensson*

Congratulations for taking a small step towards your future by stating where you want to go, being honest about where you are, and deciding what you can do to close the gap. Now it is time to take action, and I would like to help you to get the results that you desire.

CONFIDENTIALITY: As a matter of ethics, the Coach has the responsibility to maintain strict confidentiality about ALL personal information shared by the Client.

The only exception is when the Client shares information that gives the Coach reasonable cause to believe there are threats of serious harm to the Client him/herself or others. The Coach is obligated report the situation to the proper agent.

I, as Coach, promise the following:

1. All information discussed or provided during sessions will be kept strictly confidential with the exception noted above.
2. Communication will be honest and straightforward, including, asking questions and making requests.
3. My role will be to serve as a partner and champion for your success as Client.
4. An approach will be used that is in support of wholeness and balance, and where you, as Client are assumed to have the answers and be accountable for yourself.
5. I will notify you in advance to notify you if an unavoidable conflict arises so we can reschedule.
6. My Coaching role will be to ensure that the purpose of our interaction is to keep you the Client on purpose and aligned with your intentions and to support you in realizing your intentions.
7. Access to the following programs: Unleash Infinite Power Home Study, Debt Management Home Study, Strategic Marketing Blue Print, Speaker Training, Income Tax Reduction Guide, Sales Training.

You, as Client, are requested to do the following as we begin our coaching relationship:

1. Be honest. My job is to support you in those actions YOU have chosen for yourself. Please use me as a safe place to look at what stops you from being in action. 2) Make all appointments/calls on time, or call at least the day before to reschedule if an unavoidable conflict arises for you.
2. Sometimes I may ask questions which may seem too probing. Think about this right now, and decide if you can give me full permission to be bold and forthright in all our interactions.
3. Tell me what works and what doesn't work in having someone support you.
4. Affirm that you are fully responsible for the choices and decisions in your life.
5. Reflect right now to confirm whether you are absolutely certain you are ready to begin taking new opportunities and making new choices so changes in your life can happen NOW.

Thank you for completing this questionnaire.

Please email this completed document with the subject "I'm Ready To Take Action" to schedule a consultation to discuss how Ask Nate Scott Coaching can be of value to you. My email address is Nate@AskNateScott.com

As a thank-you for purchasing "Life Is Rich: How To Create Lasting Wealth", I would like to offer a scholarship for you and a family member to attend the three-day Life Is Rich Intensive Seminar as my complimentary guests. That is a total value of $3,490 - for free!

These guest seats are available for purchaser's of "Life Is Rich: How To Create Lasting Wealth" directly from my website or at an event. The course must be completed within one-year of purchase of the book and this offer is made on a space-available basis. All seating is first come, first serve. To assure your spot, please send an email to Nate@AskNateScott.com and someone will contact you with details about an upcoming event.

At the Life Is Rich Intensive weekend program, you will expand upon the insights provided in this book.

By the end of the course, you will know how to think versus what to think spiritually, mentally, emotionally, physically, and financially in order to create lasting wealth.

Whether you are currently a millionaire, middle-class, or broke, if you're not 100 percent satisfied with your income, your net worth, or your quality of life, and you have a desire for more and you are willing to take action, and then begin by sending an email to Nate@AskNateScott.com today. I guarantee that this course will educate, equip, and empower you to create a rich life.

YOU DON'T
BUILD A BUSINESS
- YOU BUILD PEOPLE -
AND THEN PEOPLE
BUILD THE BUSINESS.
-ZIG ZIGLAR

START A HOME BASED BUSINESS

For A Free Coaching Session On How To Start A
Successful Home Based Business Contact:

Place a mailing label here with
your contact information.

ABOUT THE AUTHOR

NATHANIEL SCOTT, JR., MBA, is a former enlisted soldier, war veteran, West Point Cadet, Army Ranger, and U.S. Army Captain.

After serving in the military, he worked as a contractor for three years while earning his MBA from George Washington University and completing a program in Financial Planning at Georgetown University. With degrees in hand, he entered the world of finance as a fully-licensed financial advisor and advanced to be CFO of a company listed as number 155 on INC500's fastest growing companies.

Nate is a financial engineer, business strategist, corporate leader, and sales driver offering twenty years of private sector and military leadership success.

He is poised to help you achieve measurable and tangible results in your business and life. His true value is the ability to contribute to and enhance the brain trust directing your business by structuring the organization to position it for growth, aligning the teams so they execute the strategy, and cultivating symbiotic, mutually beneficial relationships internally and externally to the business. He is a solid strategic thinker and tactical execution specialist, who formulates solutions, builds consensus, and drives performance.

He applied the same level of focus and discipline to business and Real Estate that he had successfully demonstrated in the military. The end result was the acquisition of more than a million dollars in assets in ninety days, generating $10,000 in monthly cash flow and financial independence at thirty-three.

Today, Nate is a global Internet entrepreneur, business strategist, coach, speaker, author, and CEO of NSI International, LLC.

NSI International, LLC is the preferred source of wellness-related solutions for Baby Boomers and middle-income Americans, and the preferred long-term career opportunity for new professionals dedicated to serving this expanding market. Nate's vision is "Wellness in the World: Spiritual, Mental, Emotional, Physical, and Financial."

Nate's personal mission is to live each day principle-centered based upon biblical teachings and to be a person of value and positive influence. His goal is to create a $10M endowment fund to foster personal growth and entrepreneurship because he feels those two areas, along with his faith, have had the greatest impact on his life.

Nathaniel Scott, Jr., MBA

NSI INTERNATIONAL, LLC
P.O. BOX 50223
Jacksonville Beach, FL 32240
904.838.2623
Nate@AskNateScott.com
www.AskNateScott.com
www.Facebook.com/AskNateScott